BOOK 1

Language A to Z

with David Crystal

cartoons by
Edward McLachlan

LONGMAN

Longman Group UK Limited
*Longman House, Burnt Mill, Harlow, Essex, CM20 2JE, England
and Associated Companies throughout the World.*

First published 1991
ISBN 0 582 07565 3

Set in 11/13pt Palatino Roman
Printed in Great Britain by
BPCC Hazell Books
Aylesbury, Bucks, England
Member of BPCC Ltd.

To the reader

This is a book of terms that I think are important when you're beginning to study the English language. They're listed in alphabetical order, and I've called the book an 'A to Z' – but in fact that's a bit of a cheat, because I haven't got any terms beginning with Z at all! Still, there are plenty beginning with A, to make up.

Take your time in reading the entries. I often ask you to stop and think, in the middle of an entry. Sometimes I suggest you try something out, as a little experiment. I hope you'll manage to do some of these tasks, and if you get some interesting results, let me know.

My thanks to Ben (third year) and Lucy (sixth year) for reading through the first draft of these entries, and telling me about the problems they found. Also to my wife, Hilary (who left school a few years ago), and to Brenda Howarth, John Griffin, Peter Huke, and Geoff Barton, who are still in school, teaching English in various parts of the country, and who gave me good advice about how to get the book right. And thanks too to Edward McLachlan for his marvellous cartoons.

David Crystal

Special symbols

There are four symbols used at various places in this book. This is what they mean:

Don't read this entry until you've read the entry (or entries) mentioned here. If you do, you might have a problem understanding something. I warned you!

Now that you've read this entry, you'll find that these other entries are to do with similar ideas. Have a look at them, if you want to.

You'll find that these entries in the Key Stage 4 book relate to what you've been reading.

* (as in *Go can I) This isn't an acceptable sentence in English. People don't say it or write it.

Pronunciation guide

Several entries begin with a guide to the pronunciation of a word. It's always given in brackets. What I've done is respell the word using letters which I hope will give you a clue about how the word should be said. If you're not sure what my letters mean, look in the list below.

a	is the sound of *a* in *cat*	k	is the sound of *k* in *kid*
ah	is the sound of *a* in *father*	o	is the sound of *o* in *got*
air	is the sound of *air* in *fair*	oh	is the sound of *o* in *phone*
aw	is the sound of *aw* in *saw*	oo	is the sound of *oo* in *fool*
ay	is the sound of *ay* in *say*	ow	is the sound of *ow* in *how*
e	is the sound of *e* in *get*	sh	is the sound of *sh* in *ship*
ee	is the sound of *ee* in *see*	u	is the sound of *u* in *cup*
er	is the sound of *ir* in *bird*	uh	is the sound of *a* in *sofa*
i	is the sound of *i* in *chip*	y	is the sound of *y* in *you*
ie	is the sound of *ie* in *lie*	z	is the sound of *z* in *zoo*
j	is the sound of *j* in *judge*	zh	is the sound of *s* in *television*

When you see letters printed in **bold type**, it means you should say them more loudly, when you're pronouncing the word. Practise with these:

ladder (**la**-duh)
banana (buh-**nah**-nuh)

abbreviation

Did you see Mr Fred Crumb talking about the GCSE exam during the phone-in on BBC telly last night?

It doesn't matter whether you did or not; the point is, have you noticed what's interesting about that sentence? Over a third of the words – 7 out of 19 – are **abbreviations**. An abbreviation, quite simply, is the shortened form of a word. You'll find abbreviations everywhere, and they are of many different kinds. One dictionary lists over 400,000 of them in English! The main reason for having them will be obvious if you rewrite the opening sentence in its full form:

Did you see Mister Frederick Crumb talking about the General Certificate of Secondary Education examination during the telephone-in on British Broadcasting Corporation television last night?

What a mouthful! And notice how much extra space it takes up. Using abbreviations can save you, as well as your listener or reader, a lot of time and effort. Not only this. If a group of people uses the same abbreviations, it shows they're all in the same 'gang'. And if they don't know the abbreviations, it shows they're *not* one of the gang. If Fred says, 'Smith was out l.b.w.', and Jim asks, 'What's l.b.w?', you don't need an A in English to know that Jim isn't much of a cricket fan! On the other hand, it's unwise to overuse abbreviations. Sentences can quickly become obscure if you get into the habit of putting in too many abbreviations and start talking in 'initialese'. Try this one:

The LA DJ had lost his ID, so he couldn't MC the ITV debate about NATO radar GHQ.

OK? (If not, look at the entry under **acronym**.)

 word    acronym; blend; clipping; jargon

accent

People often say things like this:

You can tell she comes from Scotland just by listening to her.
After the school trip to Paris, my friends said I came back sounding all French.

1

In the school play, Fred tried to speak like a posh nobleman, but his
voice came out like a parrot being strangled, so we couldn't
understand anything he said!
All the kids in the junior school are trying to sound like Crocodile
Dundee!

What everyone is talking about is an **accent** – the part of your voice
which tells your listeners which country you come from, or which
part of the country you come from. Of course, we don't usually
notice accents when the people speak like we do. But if newcomers
arrive in the school, their accent can stand out a mile – especially if
they come from a foreign country. Do you have any teachers with
foreign accents? Or pupils from abroad who have kept their original
accent?

Most people can tell the difference between some foreign accents.
American English is usually easy, because we hear it so much in
films. Australian, too. And even if you've never been to France,
Germany, or Spain, you'd probably recognise the accents of those
countries from the films you've seen – the French and German
voices in *'Allo 'Allo*, for instance. Listen out for the different accents
used on television in the course of an evening. If you're an accent
investigator, you have an excellent excuse for watching *Neighbours*,
Eastenders, *Coronation Street*, and the other soaps – but you have to
remember to stop listening to *what* the characters are saying and
listen instead to *how* they are saying it! People usually have

distinctive accents in comedy shows, too. And the baddies in James Bond films are generally given accents which make them sound like baddies. Accents which really stand out are often called **broad** accents.

Accents tell people which part of the country you are from. But they can sometimes tell people something about how you were educated. Listen to the way the Queen speaks, or Prince Charles, or most of the people who read the news on the radio or television. Can you tell which part of the country *they* come from? Does Prince Charles sound as if he's from Scotland? Or from Birmingham? Or from the West Country? Not a bit. He doesn't sound as if he comes from anywhere. His accent doesn't have any regional marks about it. But he does still have an accent. It's an accent which tells us something about his *social* origins – about the kind of society in which he grew up, and the kind of education he received. People sometimes call his kind of accent 'educated', 'public school', 'upper class', or just 'posh'. You'll hear it a great deal on the BBC.

 dialect; variety    articulation; Received Pronunciation

accents

If you've studied French, German, or Spanish, you'll have been struck by the small marks put over some of the letters. For instance, you can see é, è, and ê in French, ü and ö in German, and ñ in Spanish. Many languages use marks of this kind. They're called **accents**, and each has got its own name. The one you can find on è, à, and certain other letters is called a **grave accent** (pronounced grahv, to rhyme with *halve*). The one you can find on such letters as é and á goes in the other direction: it's called an **acute accent** (pronounced uh-**kyoot**). (It's easy to mix these two up, so learn a way of keeping the two names apart in your mind. Try this. The grave accent is the one that looks as if it's going down – very sad, a grave face, perhaps? The one that looks as if it's

rising up is acute – a cute smile?) The accent that looks like the roof of a house, as in ô and ê, is called a **circumflex accent** (pronounced **ser**-kuhm-fleks). The wavy line on top of a letter, such as ñ or ã, is called a **tilde** (pronounced **til**-duh, as in *Matilda*). The accent made up of two dots, as in ö and ü, is called an **umlaut** (pronounced **um**-lowt). English doesn't use accent marks, as a rule, but every now and then you'll see them, especially on words which have been borrowed from foreign languages, to help show their pronunciation. Have you noticed them on *café* and *naïve*, for instance? (You'll find some more examples if you look under **alphabet**.)

 alphabet; borrowing   diacritic

3

acronym (**ak**-ruh-nim)

The LA DJ had lost his ID, so he couldn't MC the ITV debate about NATO radar GHQ.

Or, in full:

The Los Angeles disc jockey had lost his identity card, so he couldn't be Master of Ceremonies at the Independent Television debate about the North Atlantic Treaty Organisation radar General Headquarters.

There are eight abbreviations in this sentence, and they all have one thing in common: they're all **acronyms** – words made up out of the initial letters of other words. *DJ* is an acronym of 'disc jockey'. Even *radar* is like this (if you counted only seven, you missed out *radar*): it's an acronym of 'radio detecting and ranging', but the word is so familiar nowadays that very few people know what the letters stand for. *AIDS* and *laser* are other words which are made up out of initial letters (look them up in a dictionary, if you don't know what they stand for). Acronyms are one of the commonest forms of abbreviation. Keep an eye and an ear open for them in school (are you studying *CDT* for *GCSE*?), or as you walk home (is there a *DIY*? was that a *BMW*?), read the newspapers (have you met a *VIP* or seen a *UFO*?), or watch television (*BBC* or *ITV*? a film about the *FBI* or *CIA*?). But beware: have you noticed that *TV* and *HQ* are different? Sometimes acronyms cheat, and use letters from *inside* the word as well!

abbreviation; word

acrostic (uh-**kros**-tik)

An **acrostic** is a kind of word game. The basic idea is very simple: you write a series of short lines, so that the first letter of each line spells out a word or phrase.

Here's an example
Of an acrostic
That I just made up.

The acrostic is HOT. Now let's make things trickier. Try writing one where the meaning of the acrostic sums up what the lines are all about.

Forehead,
A mouth and nose,
Chin and cheeks,
Eyes and ears.

No problem with FACE? Then try this: write one as a poem, with the lines *rhyming*. Or this: turn one into a puzzle, making each line a clue (like a crossword puzzle clue), and put the acrostic letters into the *answer*! Or do both at once:

Clues	Answers
Colour in trees	Brown
Looking around	Eyes
Kept in a zoo	Animal
A powerful sound	Roar

Did you get BEAR? And if you're really smart, you can go for a 'triple' acrostic, with a letter in the *middle* of each line making up a word as well.

 anagram; palindrome; pangram; rebus; riddle

adjective (**ad**-juhk-tiv)

Here's how someone described a car accident the other day:

. . . so anyway, this big green car was going along the inside lane of the main road, when this red sports car pulled out of a side road and went into it – there was a loud bang and a terrible scraping noise . . .

Here's how he *didn't* tell the story:

. . . so anyway, this car was going along the lane of the road, when this car pulled out from a road and went into it – there was a bang and a noise . . .

You can see why. It's a much more boring version. It hardly paints a picture of what happened, in the way the first version does. And it doesn't even make much sense, in places: 'the lane of the road'? 'a bang and a noise'?

What's the difference between the two versions? Look at the words which have been left out: *big, green, inside, main, red, sports, side, loud, terrible, scraping.* These words all have the same job to do: they add the important details. If you were a witness, it wouldn't be any

5

good telling the police that 'a car hit a car', just giving the nouns and nothing else. They'd want a bit more information than that – something like 'the red sports car hit the big green car'. In grammar, words which describe nouns are called **adjectives**.

There are four chief ways to tell an adjective. Most adjectives can be used in front of a noun, following words like *the* or *a*: all the adjectives in the accident story do that. In addition, most adjectives can be used on their own, after a verb like *is* or *are*. So, you can say both *the red car* and *the car is red*. You can also put words like *very* in front of most adjectives: *a very loud bang*. And you can use adjectives to make comparisons, sometimes by adding the endings *-er* or *-est*, sometimes by using the words *more* and *most*. *Big, bigger, biggest*. *Ridiculous, more ridiculous, most ridiculous*. If a word does all four of these things, it's definitely an adjective. Use these clues to go adjective-hunting, and see how many you find. (But beware! Not all adjectives work in exactly the same way. For instance, if you put *very* in front of each adjective in the accident story, you'll find that the result sometimes sounds like good English (*very big car*) and sometimes it doesn't (**very scraping noise*). So, when you're being an adjective detective, be prepared to meet adjectives of several different kinds.)

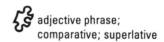 noun; parts of speech   adjective phrase; comparative; superlative

 irregular

adjective phrase

Sometimes, adjectives can be used on their own, without being attached to any noun. *Great!*, you might say, if somebody told you the school was having an extra holiday. *Awful!*, you might say, if you then discovered that the person who told you the news was lying! When adjectives are used like this, you can usually add other words to them, to sharpen the meaning or make it come across more strongly. *Blinking awful!*, you might say (and I imagine you can think of a few other words to use instead of *blinking – rather*

and *jolly*, for instance). Phrases like these are called **adjective phrases**, because the main word in the phrase is an adjective. Some more examples? Try these: *jolly good, terribly loud, a bit unhappy, most interesting, more valuable, really brilliant, technically impossible, very nice, very very nice, very very very nice . . .* And of course, any of these phrases can be used in a sentence too: *That's very nice, That book is really interesting*.

 adjective; phrase   noun phrase

adverb (ad-verb)

... Smith passes beautifully to Gray, who heads it very firmly and deliberately to Pritchard, who pushes it nimbly towards the post. Jones is there, waiting patiently, and now he's got a chance – and he shoots, and yes it's there!!! – Just as the half-time whistle goes. Well, Jones has played really brilliantly in this match ...

We can take a break there, because it's half-time. Of course, to get the full effect of a piece of football commentary, you really have to listen to it. But even on the page, some of the drama comes across. Which words carry the atmosphere? You can tell, if you rewrite the first sentence leaving out the vivid words:

... Smith passes to Gray, who heads it to Pritchard, who pushes it towards the post.

I could think of some vivid words to describe your goalkeeping

Words like *beautifully*, *very firmly*, *deliberately*, and *nimbly* help to paint the picture, and they all have one thing in common: they tell you *how* the actions were carried out. If you read the rest of the passage, you'll find two more. Without them, the commentary sounds distinctly dull. The verbs by themselves have no impact. It's likely that any sports commentator who left them out wouldn't be a sports commentator for very long!

A word which gives you further details about the action of a verb is called an **adverb**. Words like *firmly* and *nimbly* are called **adverbs of manner**, because they tell you the 'manner' of the action – 'how' it happened. If the adverbs tell you 'when' the action took place, they are called **adverbs of time**: these include *today*, *yesterday*, *then*, and *now*. If they tell you 'where' the action took place, they are called **adverbs of place**: these include *here*, *there*, *upstairs*, and *outside*. These are the commonest kinds of adverb.

There are also a few other kinds of adverb which don't have anything to do with verbs. For instance, *very* and *really* add extra strength to the meaning of the next word (*really strong, very quickly*). Words like *however* and *moreover* join sentences together. They're all thought of as kinds of adverb.

By the way, have you noticed that most adverbs end in *-ly*? Adverbs like *soon* and *now* and *however* are some of the exceptions. The usual way to make an adverb is to take an adjective and add *-ly* to it. Try it. *Quick? Quickly. Beautiful? Beautifully. Sad? Sadly.* But beware! Not all adjectives allow this to happen, and sometimes when they do, you end up with a very different meaning. *Fast – fastly?* Hardly!

 verb    adjective; adverbial; adverb phrase

adverbial (ad-**ver**-bee-uhl)

You know what adverbs are. (I hope. If not, you'd better read the **adverb** entry now.) Here's a sentence containing a time adverb:

Ermintrude is leaving today.

When is she leaving? Today. But there are other ways of answering this 'when'-question. When is she leaving?

Ermintrude is leaving at three o'clock.
                    very soon.
                    when the clock strikes three.
                    after she's eaten her lunch.

All of these constructions tell you when the event will take place, but the first two are phrases and the last two are clauses. It's handy to have a name for *all* the constructions that do the job of an adverb, and this name is **adverbial**. So, *at three o'clock* and *very soon* are examples of **adverbial phrases**, and *when the clock strikes three* and *after she's eaten her lunch* are examples of **adverbial clauses**. Here's a diagram which sums up the three kinds of adverbial.

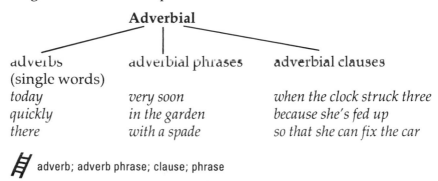

Adverbial

adverbs (single words)	adverbial phrases	adverbial clauses
today	*very soon*	*when the clock struck three*
quickly	*in the garden*	*because she's fed up*
there	*with a spade*	*so that she can fix the car*

 adverb; adverb phrase; clause; phrase

adverb phrase

Do you remember the entry on **adverb**? An adverb is a single word (such as *happily* or *now*), but quite often we use another word along with it, to give extra emphasis or a new slant to the meaning. *Very happily* or *right now*, for instance. These are called **adverb phrases**. They're 'phrases' because they've got more than one word inside them; and they're 'adverb' phrases because the important word in the phrase is the adverb. (You can tell which is the most important word because, if you leave it out, the phrase doesn't make much sense. Try this test. You can say *The burglar moved very carefully*. You can also say *The burglar moved carefully*. But you can't say **The burglar moved very*. This shows that *carefully* is a more important word than *very* in this sentence.) Some other adverb phrases are *just then*, *more carefully*, *very kindly*, and *right there*. There's another adverb phrase in the second sentence of this entry, too. Can you find it?

 adverb; phrase    prepositional phrase

9

affirmative (uh-**ferm**-uh-tiv)

You've probably seen films where people are talking to each other over the radio – pilots, astronauts, or soldiers, for example. Have you noticed that they often don't say a simple *yes* and *no*, when they reply to a question, but *affirmative* (for 'yes') and *negative* (for 'no')? These words have the same sort of meaning when you're talking about language. An **affirmative sentence** is one where you are saying 'yes' about what happens. It's different from a **negative sentence**, which says 'no' about what happens. You can easily tell the difference in English, because negative sentences usually have the word *not* inside them – or the shortened form of *not*, which is *n't*. *Not* usually goes very close to the verb. *n't* can't get any closer: it's always a verb ending.

Affirmative sentences	*Negative sentences*
Your parrot has been sick.	My parrot has not been sick.
I think we're lost.	I don't think we're lost.
Veronica can ride a bike.	Veronica can't ride a bike.

The word **positive** is often used instead of affirmative. I'm positive.

sentence; verb   negative; statement

affix (**a**-fiks)
affixation (a-fik-**say**-shuhn)

Have you ever wondered, 'What's the longest word in the English language?' People sometimes say *antidisestablishmentarianism*. (If they do, they're wrong. It's only got 28 letters. Someone has found a word of 36 letters in *Webster's Third International Dictionary*. Try saying *praetertransubstantiationalistically*. But don't ask me what it means!)

So, how do you make words longer and longer? The usual way is to add bits of extra meaning at the beginning and at the end, and these are called **affixes**. You start with a simple word, like *pig*, *soap*, or (in the long words you've just seen) *establish* and *substance*. The affixes you add at the beginning are called **prefixes**; the affixes you add at the end are called **suffixes**. Common prefixes are *dis-*, *un-*, *mega-*, *super-*, *anti-*, and *tele-*. Common suffixes are *-s*, *-ness*, *-ful*, *-ing*, *-ism*, and *-ation*. Each one changes the meaning of the word in some way. *Un-* usually means 'not', for instance; *mega-* means 'great'. Try

working out which are the affixes in *antidis . . .* You should find two prefixes and three suffixes. Check each one out by finding other words which make use of the same affix, and see if you can work out what its meaning is. For instance, if you picked *anti-*, you could find *anti-aircraft gun, anti-tank gun* and *anti-freeze*, and you could guess that the meaning of *anti-* is 'against'. Mind you, you can't add prefixes and suffixes any way you want. There are rules which you have to follow, and there are lots of exceptions. We say *unhappy* but not *unsad*, for example.

You can play with affixes, if you like, inventing your own new words. What about *desoapification*, for the state of someone who doesn't like washing? Or *uncomicness*, to describe the state of someone who has just lost all his comics? Who knows? Some of them might catch on.

 word   root    morphology

agreement see **concord**

alphabet

What is there to say about the **alphabet** that you don't know already? It's hardly the most exciting of subjects. You've lived with it for too long. You know it by heart (forwards, at least – but have you tried saying it backwards?). So, you'll be able to answer three simple questions about it, then? Write down your answers, before you read on.

1 How many different letter shapes are there in the alphabet?
2 Which are the five most frequently used letters, and which are the five least frequently used?
3 Can you think of any 'foreign' letters which don't belong in the basic set of 26, but which are sometimes used in English?

Now, some answers.

● What did you get for the number of different letter shapes? If you thought 26, you're wrong. I asked for 'letter *shapes*', not 'letters'. 52, then? That would be 26 capital letters ('upper-case' letters, printers call them) and 26 small letters ('lower-case letters'). Still wrong. The answer is 44. Work it out. *A* is different from *a*, *B* is different from *b*, *C* and *c* are the same, and so on. In fact, there are only 8 letters which are identical in their upper-case and lower-case forms: C, O, P, S, V, W, X, Z. That leaves 18 upper-case letters, their 18 lower-case partners, and the 8 identical ones: 44.

● You'll have to do a piece of research to answer the second question correctly. Here's what you do. Make a list of all the letters in the alphabet, then choose a page of this book. Next, go through the page,

Honestly – all I did was recite the alphabet backwards

letter by letter, and each time a letter occurs, put a tick against the corresponding letter in your list. Then count up. *E* will be the commonest. But what comes next?

• Now for the 'foreign' letters. There aren't very many, and they don't turn up very often, but when they do, you need to know what to do with them. For instance, you'll sometimes find two letters joined together to make a single letter, as in the old-fashioned spellings of certain learnèd words, such as *encyclopædia* or *œsophagus*. You won't come across these very often. More important are the letters which make use of an accent mark. These are usually words which have been taken over by English from some other language where accent marks are normal. Most of them come from French – such as *fête*, *café*, *soufflé*, *naïve*, and *résumé*. Sometimes these accents have a real job to do: they give you a clue about how to pronounce the word. (Did you notice how I spelled the word *learnèd* just now, pronounced **ler**-ned, to distinguish it from the verb *learned*, as in *My cousin's learned to drive a car*?) But sometimes accents are just there for show – making the English seem special by adding a hint of the foreign language. If you go to a posh restaurant, you'll probably find several accent marks in the menu. And next time you're walking through a big store, look at the perfume counter.

 accent; logogram; punctuation; upper case

ambiguous (am-**big**-yoo-uhs)
ambiguity (am-big-**yoo**-i-tee)

GIANT WAVES IN BLACKPOOL

Read all about it! But, read all about *what*? About gale-force winds driving the sea onto the prom? Probably. Or maybe it's an even better story, about a Huge Friendly Being sighted above the Tower. Whatever the writer intended, that headline has got two meanings. We say it's **ambiguous**. A piece of language is ambiguous when it can be taken in more than one way. It's not a problem for *you* – you know what you meant. It's a problem for your listener or reader, who can't work out what you were getting at. Indeed, some sentences can be ambiguous in more than two ways. You can get *four* meanings out of this one, if you really try hard:

The inspector ordered the policeman to stop drinking at four o'clock.
(Who's doing the drinking? The policeman? or someone else?
And what happened at four o'clock? The drinking? or the ordering?)

By contrast, here's a nice simple ambiguity:

There's a hot dog in the front room.
(Will you stroke it? or eat it?)

This one is ambiguous only when you say it aloud:

Your tremendous feat/feet should be in the newspaper.

The spelling makes it clear.

And this one is ambiguous only when you read it:

There were tears everywhere.
(Were the faces sad? Or were the clothes torn?)

Ambiguities can waste a lot of time and be very misleading. It's a sensible policy, especially when you're writing, to try to avoid them.

 polysemic

anagram (**an**-uh-gram)

When you take a word or phrase, and turn all its letters round so that you get another word or phrase, you've got an **anagram**. For instance:

disease is an anagram of *seaside* (or the other way round, of course)
canter, *nectar*, and *trance* are all anagrams of each other

If you've ever done a crossword puzzle, you've probably had to cope with an anagram or two. Do you remember a clue like this?

4 Down. You'll need a doctor if there's a mix-up at the seaside. (7 letters)

To solve this clue, you have to take the hint that 'mix-up' means 'change the letters around in one of the words in the clue'. So, if you rearrange the seven letters of *seaside*, you'll get a word which has the meaning to do with needing a doctor – and the answer is *disease*. People spend a lot of time looking for really clever anagrams. Did you know that *astronomers* is an anagram of *moon-starers*? Or that *mother-in-law* is an anagram of *woman Hitler*? You can try doing this yourself. Take a famous name, and see whether its letters make an interesting anagram. People have done this to *Margaret Thatcher*, for example, and produced *Meg the arch tartar* and *that great charmer*! But be prepared to spend a bit of time at it. Finding out whether you can get an anagram from a word or phrase isn't always easy. There are three anagrams of the word *regal*, for instance. Can you find them? Too easy? All right, try this: find two anagrams out of *garden* (using *all* the letters, remember).

 word games

antonyms (**an**-tuh-nimz)
antonymy (an-**ton**-uh-mee)

When two words have opposite meanings, we call them **antonyms**. So, *fat* is the antonym of *thin*, and *thin* is the antonym of *fat*. *Happy* is the opposite of *sad*, and *sad* is the opposite of *happy*. Enough said? Not quite. If all the opposites in English were like this, the entry would stop here. I'm afraid they're not. Take a look at this pair of antonyms: *single – married*. How do they differ from *fat – thin*? The important point about *fat* and *thin* is that they are at two ends of a scale. At one end of the scale, you can imagine someone who's enormously fat, then someone who's not quite so fat, then someone who's only slightly fat, and so on. At the other end of the scale, there are people who are extremely thin, and others who aren't quite so thin. In the middle, there are people who are neither fat nor thin. So, we can say in English: *That dog's fat, That one's very fat*, and *That one's very very fat*. Or, *Rover's fatter than Fido* or *He's fattest of all*. But you can't talk like this with *single* and *married*. We don't say *He's very single, He's very very single*, or *John's more single than Jim* – though I suppose you could make a joke and say 'Look at that hen-pecked husband. He looks very married!' *Single* and *married* aren't at either end of a scale of 'marriedness', whereas *fat* and *thin* are at either end of a scale of 'fatness'. We call antonyms like *fat* and *thin* **gradable**, and those like *single* and *married* **ungradable**. Can you think of any more ungradable ones? Try *freed prisoners* and *captured prisoners*.

 synonyms   hyponyms

apostrophe (uh-**pos**-truh-free)

What have *I'm tired, He isn't, Fred's skateboard, three o'clock,* and *cross your t's* got in common? Easy. They're all using the punctuation mark called an **apostrophe**. What's not quite so easy is to work out why the apostrophe is there at all. What's it for?

In most cases, the apostrophe shows you that a letter has been left out: so, *I'm* is short for *I am,* and *isn't* is short for *is not.* Other cases like this are *he's, it's, can't,* and *you're.* Sometimes, it shows that a sound has been left out in casual speech: *I'm goin' huntin', shootin', and fishin'.* The quick way of saying *because* is *'cos,* and this is usually written with an apostrophe, to show that part of the normal spelling has been left out. And people often write things like *in '81,* for *in 1981.* But in cases like *Fred's skateboard,* nothing has been left out. Here, the apostrophe is telling you that the *s* attached to *Fred* means 'belonging to'. The skateboard belongs to Fred. Why do we need an apostrophe here? If we didn't have one, it could be a bit confusing, as the *s* would look like a plural ending. Compare *Fred's* and *Freds.* The first one means: 'something belongs to Fred'. The second one means: 'lots of people called Fred'. Look at this one: *Have you met my cousin's brother's daughter?* Without the apostrophe it would look weird: *Have you met my cousins brothers daughter?* That's the reason why you get an apostrophe in *cross the t's,* by the way. To write *cross the ts* would look very odd – as would *dot your is*!

 punctuation    case; contraction

appropriate

Do you have a wardrobe at home? If so, take a look in it. You'll see a whole range of clothes – some for smart occasions, some for everyday, some for school, and some for messy jobs. You don't use them without thinking about it. You know that clothing suitable for one occasion may be quite unsuitable for another. A swimming costume is appropriate for the seaside or the pool, but not for going to the cinema or going to church. Your school may have strong opinions about what sort of clothes it's appropriate to wear – are you in uniform now? If you've been to a wedding, you'll know that the clothes people wear are a very important part of the occasion. If you get your choice of clothes wrong, it can be very embarrassing. Some people spend hours deciding what to wear before they show their faces outside. Do you know someone like that?

Language is a bit like this. When you learn a language, you learn all kinds of styles of speaking and writing. It's a process that goes on all your life, and it starts at a very early age, when parents teach their children how to be polite. I've heard parents say things like this, to children of around four years of age:

Don't talk like that to your father!
Don't shout! It's rude.
Don't talk with your mouth full!
Go and wash your mouth out with soap!

Speaking politely is just one of many styles that we have to learn, as we become expert in English. These styles of language are similar to styles of clothing: we judge them to be **appropriate** or **inappropriate** to different circumstances. For instance, people write more carefully when they don't know the person they're writing to. They speak more politely when addressing strangers or superiors. Radio announcers speak more slowly when they're on the air than when they're chatting in the canteen. Lawyers talk differently when they make a case in court and when they're with their families. Students don't use the same language to their teachers as they do to their mates – at least, not usually!

 audience; colloquial speech; correctness; formal; style

archaism (**ah**-kay-izm)
archaic (ah-**kay**-ik)

Lo! Get thee gone. The milkman hath been, and thou art late for school.

If any mother spoke like this to her child in the morning, the child could be forgiven for thinking, 'That's it! She's finally snapped!' People don't usually speak like this – or, at least, they don't nowadays. Some of the words and constructions are distinctly odd – the greeting *Lo!*, the words *thou* (instead of 'you') and *art* (instead of 'are'), endings like *-th* instead of *-s* (*hath* for 'has'), and the construction *Get thee gone*. These forms are **archaisms**: they were used in the language a long time ago, and are now used only to give an old-fashioned or high-sounding tone. You may have seen some of these words if you've read poems, stories, or plays which were written long ago, or which have been written about olden times. If you have a comic telling the story of Robin Hood or King Arthur, for instance, the dialogue will be peppered with words like *forsooth* and *varlet*, to give an old-fashioned flavour to the language. You can also find archaic words in fairy stories and nursery rhymes. And

sometimes you'll even hear archaic words in speech, especially if you go to church. *Our Father, which art in heaven, hallowed by thy name . . .*

 vocabulary   etymology; neologism

article (**ah**-ti-kuhl)

We usually talk about 'articles of clothing' or 'articles in a newspaper'. It's strange to find this term used to describe a type of word in the grammar of a language. But, don't be fooled by the strange name: the **article** has a very special job to do. In fact, there are *two* articles in English: *the* and *a*. *The* is the commonest word in the language, and *a* isn't far behind. Notice that you can't use them on their own: to say *the*, by itself, wouldn't make any kind of sense. The articles have got to be accompanied by a noun: *the cat* or *a cat* begins to make some sense. So, what's the difference between them?

A is called the **indefinite article**, because it leaves the identity of the noun it goes with unclear, or 'indefinite'. Think about this sentence: *A cat was sitting on a car*. Which cat, exactly? Which car? You don't know. All you know is that some cat or other was sitting on some car or other. The indefinite meaning is signalled by the word *a*. Now, compare that sentence with this one: *The cat was sitting on the car*. This time, the meaning is more specific, or definite: **the** cat (you know, the one we were talking about earlier) was sitting on **the** car (you know, the one we were talking about earlier). Because *the* conveys a more definite impression, it's called the **definite article**.

There are some important differences between the two words. *A* can be used only with singular nouns: you can't say **a cats*. *The* can be used with either singular or plural nouns: you can say both *the cat* and *the cats*. Most nouns can be used with either *a* or *the* – but some can't take *a* (you can't say **a mud* or **a fun*, for instance). And here's an interesting thought. Sometimes it's important *not* to use any article at all, to express a particular meaning. Think of the difference between *I'd like a/the cake* and *I like cake*. In the first sentence, you're thinking of a single cake. In the second sentence, you mean just 'cake – of any kind'. In language, when you *don't* say something, it's sometimes as important as when you do.

 noun   ² determiner

audience

If you go to a cinema, or a theatre, you're a member of the **audience**. Everyone else does the work, and you just sit back and enjoy it. When you use language, you have to think of the audience too – *your* audience. Who's listening to you? Who's going to read what you write? This time, *you* have to do the work. It's very important to think of these people before you start communicating. If you don't, you might choose the wrong kind of language and end up making a fool of yourself – as well as upsetting someone else into the bargain. For instance, imagine you're writing a letter to apply for a part-time job to Miss Mabel Spanner, who runs a local newsagent's. How will you begin your letter?

How's tricks, Mabel me old love?   Dear Spanner
Dear Miss Spanner   Dear Miss Mabel Spanner
Dear Miss Mabel   Mabelkins
'Ere, Spanner!

There are a few other options open to you, but I'd go for 'Dear Miss Spanner' myself – that's if I really wanted the job! On the other hand, if you're writing to an old friend, there'd be no harm at all in starting off with a 'How's tricks?' This time, it's the 'Dear Mr' form which would look odd. Stories of this kind show how important it is to think of your audience when you're writing or speaking to someone. And the more people you're communicating with, the more careful you have to be. It's tricky enough deciding how to talk to *one* person. Imagine what it's like talking to dozens (as when someone gives a speech) or even millions (as when people talk on the radio, or write in the newspaper). Now that's a *real* audience!

 appropriate; communication; style; variety   context

auxiliary verb (og-**zil**-yuh-ree verb) and main verb

A boy comes up to you and says, *I growl.* He then says, *I am growling, I have been growling, I might growl, I can growl, I must growl, I do growl,* and *I shall growl.* What do you think of this (after you've called the men in white coats to come and take him away)? As a grammarian, you should notice that there are two kinds of verb in these sentences. The verb which carries most of the meaning is *growl*, obviously: that's the **main verb** in each sentence. The other verbs are *am*, *have been*, *might*, *can*, *must*, *do*, and *shall*. These verbs aren't quite so crucial. Their job is to add something to the meaning of the main verb. Is the speaker growling now, in the past, or in the future? Is he growling for a short time or a long time? Is he definitely going to growl, or only possibly? Verbs which add meanings like this are called **auxiliary verbs**, or **auxiliaries**, for short.

There aren't very many auxiliaries in English, but they are used very frequently. The various forms of *be* and *have* are especially important, because they express such important meanings as the time of the action and how long it went on for – think about the difference between *I am growling* (now), *I have been growling* (for the past five minutes), and *I was growling* (yesterday). The forms of *do* are used to express emphasis (*I do growl* – stamping your foot!) and to ask questions (*Do I growl?*). The auxiliaries *can*, *could*, *may*, *might*, *will*, *would*, *shall*, *should*, and *must* tell you whether something is possible or likely or necessary. These are called the **modal auxiliaries**, because they express a range of attitudes, or moods. And there are a few other verbs, like *need* and *ought*, which also work in an auxiliary way. If you study how auxiliary verbs are used in sentences, you'll find that they're not at all like main verbs. For instance, they can go at the beginning of a sentence, when you're asking a question – *Is he eating?*, *Can I leave?* Main verbs can't. You can't say **Eats he?* or **Leave I?*

By the way, sometimes an auxiliary verb can be used *without* its main verb. In a shortened sentence, you'll find this sort of thing:

ENA: John can drink 12 pints of milk at one go.
LENA: He can't.
ENA: He really can.

You can keep that conversation going for ages, just using auxiliary verbs, if you want.

LENA: He shouldn't.
ENA: He does.
LENA: He musn't.
ENA: He will.

Of course, if you come in half way through such a conversation, you've no idea what everyone's talking about!

 verb   mood

baby talk

This little phrase has two meanings. First of all, it refers to the distinctive way babies talk, when they're learning to speak – from around 12 months of age until they're about two or three. They say such things as *goggie* for 'dog' or *mama* for 'mother', and such sentences as *me kick ball* and *teddy allgone*. But **baby talk** has a more important meaning, in studies of children's language. It also describes the speech of people when they talk *to* little children. These people use baby words, such as *doggie*, *horsie*, and *choo-choo*. They use baby sentences, such as *bye-bye daddy's car*. And they use baby pronunciations, such as *dem* for 'them'. *Who's a lovely ickle baba, den?* They sound totally stupid, in fact. Or perhaps I should say 'we' – because we all do it.

(Oh, I almost forgot. Have you noticed that people use baby talk not only when they're talking to babies? Listen the next time someone talks to their pet cat or pet budgie, and you'll see what I mean!)

 motherese   holophrase

back slang

Here's a challenge. How quickly can you take a sentence and say it so that each word in it is pronounced backwards? Try *The cat sat on the mat*. It should sound something like *Et tac tas no et tam*. This is an ancient kind of word game, called **back slang**. Sometimes, just the main words are pronounced backwards – as in *The tac tas on the tam*. Back slang has been used by children, shopkeepers, thieves, barrow-boys, and many others. It was usually done for fun, but often it was a way of keeping a message secret. Some people have learned to talk like this at great speed. But it gets very tricky doing fast back slang when the words are long. Practise saying *intelligence, military operations*, and *weather forecast* backwards, and you'll see what I mean. A slow process, isn't it!

 slang; word games

bilingual (bie-**ling**-gwuhl)

A bi-cycle has got two wheels. A bi-plane has got two sets of wings. A bilingual has got two – ?

Languages. Anyone who speaks two languages fluently is said to be **bilingual**. (Actually, if you speak *more* than two languages, you're still called bilingual – not 'trilingual' or 'quadrilingual', or whatever.) Countries which regularly use more than one language are **multilingual** – Belgium, Switzerland, India, Ghana, and many more. If you live in Britain, of course, you probably won't meet many bilinguals. Most of the people of England, Wales, Scotland, and Northern Ireland speak only one language – they're **monolingual**. The main exceptions are those in Wales who speak Welsh, and those in Scotland who speak Gaelic, in addition to English. And of course, there are a large number of people who have come from abroad to live in this country, many of whom speak their own language as well as English. But still, most British people are monolingual, and don't seem to be terribly bothered about learning another language well. This is a great shame. It's marvellous to be able to speak a second language so that you can really join in with people from another culture – even if you're only on holiday in their country for a couple of weeks. And it can be very useful, too, especially if you have to do business abroad, or want to feel the impact of poems and stories written in their original language. Nobody knows just how many bilingual people there are in the world, but my guess is that well over two-thirds of the people on earth know at least two languages. So, here in Britain we're among the odd ones out.

 language

blend

Have you ever had brunch? Or been to a heliport? Or listened to a newscast? Do you know of anyone who's been breathalysed? or electrocuted? Did you ever watch a programme about a bionic man or about Interpol? Why am I asking all these questions? Because all of these words are examples of **blends** – words which are made up by combining bits of other words, usually the first part of one word and the last part of another. So, *brunch* is a blend of *breakfast* and *lunch*. *Newscast* is a blend of *news* and *broadcast*. *Bionic = biological + electronic. Interpol = international + police*. Can you work out the others?

 word    abbreviation; clipping

block language

WAY OUT	*The Sun*	30 mph
For Sale	KEEP OFF THE GRASS	English Department
No smoking	New improved Bloggo!!	DOG BITES POSTMAN

What have all these bits of language got in common? Think of where you'd see them. They're notices, signs, labels, headlines, titles, advertisements . . . They're all cases where the writer wants to send a short, sharp message, so the sentences don't have their usual filled-out look. You get *Dog bites postman* in a newspaper headline, not *A dog has bitten a postman*. Try working out the missing bits of language. *(This is the) WAY OUT? (This house is) For Sale*? You don't need the missing bits, because the language has a fixed structure to it, and everyone understands what it means. Language of this kind is often called **block language**, because you take the language as a single chunk, or block, and you don't need to analyse it into bits. Many of these sentences are like a formula which you learn off by heart. You don't ever *read* the name of a newspaper, for instance. You simply learn to recognise it. Or, if you're walking in the park, and you see a sign sticking up in the middle of a lawn, you automatically think 'It probably says *Keep off*'. You'd be rather surprised, when you got nearer, if it said 'Don't you think that poetry is a wonderful thing?'

By the way, you can sometimes find block language in speech, too. Listen to the news headlines on radio or TV, for instance. They often copy the newspaper style. And when you next say *Happy birthday* or *Merry Christmas*, you're talking in block language.

 formula

body language see **communication**

borrowing or loan word

You lend things and borrow things – and so do languages. When languages meet, they borrow words from each other – or perhaps 'copy' would be a better term, because the words end up in both! English has borrowed thousands of words from other languages over the centuries. And other languages have borrowed many words from English, too. If you go to France, you'll hear people talking about *le weekend* and *le computer*. Here are a few examples of **loan words** or **borrowings** that have come into English, along with the name of the language the words came from:

algebra	Arabic	*robot*	Czech
anorak	Eskimo	*sauna*	Finnish
banana	Spanish	*slim*	Dutch
crag	Welsh	*sofa*	Persian
equator	Latin	*studio*	Italian
hamster	German	*swastika*	Sanskrit
ketchup	Chinese	*thug*	Hindi
marmalade	Portuguese	*trek*	Afrikaans
medicine	French	*tycoon*	Japanese
pylon	Greek	*yoghurt*	Turkish

Any largish dictionary will tell you where a word comes from.

 word   dictionary; etymology

brackets or parentheses (puh-**ren**-thuh-seez)

There's an example, straight away. Where? There, just above. **Parentheses** are used to set a piece of language off from the rest of the text – to show that it's separate, in some way. I've just used them to show you that the pronunciation guide is an extra bit of information. In British English, they're usually simply called **brackets**. In fact there are three kinds of brackets used in written English. **Round brackets** are the common ones, and they're shown above. **Square brackets** look like this: [ ]. 'Curly brackets', or **braces**, are often used in scientific writing, and they look like this: { }. You chiefly use brackets when you want to add an extra remark to a sentence without disturbing your main line of thought. Your sentence starts off; then, at a certain point you decide to say a bit more about something, just as I'm doing now (I am the author, after all, so I can write this sentence how I like). Notice that if you leave out the language inside the brackets, you still have a complete sentence.

It's wise never to overuse brackets. It can get very confusing if you have several sets in a row, or put brackets inside other brackets. If you don't believe me, see if you can work this sentence out:

John (my uncle (who lives in Reading (near the station))) met John (my brother (who's just come back from abroad (France))) in the High Street.

Try collecting examples of the ways in which brackets are used. Here are some examples to start you off:

(1) Henry VIII (1491–1547)
(2) water (H_2O)
(3) Jim Smith (England)
(4) Republic of Korea (South Korea)

(And don't forget the example at the beginning of this entry.)
(Or this one, at the end.)

 punctuation

capital letter see **upper case**

case

A girl saw a girl in the park.
She saw her in the park.

Look at these rather weird sentences closely. The only difference
between them is that two personal pronouns have replaced two
noun phrases (*a girl*). But wait a moment. Why are there *different*
feminine pronouns in the second sentence? Why can't it be 'She saw
she in the park'? Or 'Her saw her in the park'? That's just the way it
is, I'm afraid. That's the way the language works. Because of the
way the English language developed, hundreds of years ago, we are
left with more than one form of the feminine pronoun. You use the
she form when the pronoun acts as the subject of a sentence, and
you use the *her* form when it acts as the object. There's also another
feminine form which you use when you want to express the idea of
possession – *hers*. These variations in the form of a word show
the job that the word is doing in the sentence. They're called **cases**.

I've shown you three cases, so far. The *she* form is called the
subjective case, because it's the form you have to use when the
word acts as subject of a sentence. The *her* form is called the
objective case, because it's the case you have to use when the word
acts as object. And the *hers* form is called the **possessive** or **genitive
case**, because it's the case you have to use when you want to express
the idea of 'belonging to'. (*Genitive* is a strange-looking term. It was
originally a Latin word, meaning 'of birth'. The early grammar-book
writers used it when they tried to describe the 'belonging to' idea.)

All the personal pronouns have a subjective case (*I, you, he, she, it, we, they*). All of them have a possessive case, too (*mine, yours, his, hers, its, ours, theirs*). But not all of them have an objective case: *you* and *it* don't. Try them out. *You saw John, John saw you – you* is the same in both sentences). *It fell, I broke it* (no change for *it* either).

Do any other parts of speech have endings which show the role they play in the sentence? Adjectives don't change their form when they move from one part of the sentence to another. Nor do adverbs . . . But nouns? A long time ago, in English, nouns had all kinds of case endings. These days, there's only one ending left: the genitive – the one that shows possession.

my uncle's car   the dog's bone

We can't say *my uncle car or *the dog bone. We have to use the 'apostrophe *s*' ending, when we're writing (and add *s* sounds when we speak). It's sometimes called the 'genitive *s*' ending. If the noun doing the possessing is in the singular, you have to put the apostrophe before the *s*. If it's in the plural (there's more than one), you have to put it after the *s* – like this:

my uncles' car (meaning, the car belonging to all my uncles)
the dogs' bones (meaning, the bones belonging to several dogs)

This has been quite a long entry. I think I'd better stop now, before we all turn into cases ourselves.

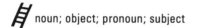 noun; object; pronoun; subject   number

circumlocution (ser-kuhm-loh-**kyoo**-shuhn)

Toni moved one foot in front of the other foot and went in the general direction of the building where the buses begin their journeys.

Or, putting it another way, 'Toni walked towards the bus station'. You can see what's happened. The first version has 25 words. The second has 6. When someone says or writes something in a roundabout way, using more words than they need in order to express their meaning, it's called **circumlocution** or **periphrasis** (puh-**ri**-fruh-sis). People don't usually like circumlocutions. 'Get to the point', they say. And generally, in English, it's wise not to use two words if one will do. Of course, some people make a habit of using circumlocutions. Listen to the next time a politician is asked a

straight question, and see how many circumlocutions you can count
in the answer.

REPORTER: Did you have an argument with the Prime Minister?
POLITICIAN: I think it's probably true to say that we had an
interesting and constructive exchange of views.

In other words: Yes!

cliche; diction; jargon

clause (klawz)

When you start a sentence, you can go on for ever if you want to.
Some people do.

I went to town on the bus the other day and on the way I met Fred
and Fred had his friend Abdul with him and so I said to him . . . and
he said to me . . . and I said . . . and he said . . .

If you want to describe the structure of an utterance like this, the
word 'sentence' isn't much use, because the whole thing is one
enormous sentence (we haven't reached a full stop yet, remember).
But you can probably see how this sentence breaks down into
smaller chunks. Here are some of them:

I went to town on the bus the other day
on the way I met Fred
Fred had his friend Abdul with him

These smaller pieces are called **clauses**. You can have any number of clauses in a sentence. Or there might be just one:

I can see a toad.
Make my day!
That man's got chewing gum in his ear.

Clauses join together in different ways (see the entries on **coordination** and **subordination** to find out what these are). You can also analyse a clause into its parts, or **elements**, and look at the way these elements make up different patterns. There aren't many clause patterns possible in English – but that's another story (see **clause analysis**).

sentence   clause analysis; coordination; subordination

clause analysis

How many ways are there of putting words together to make a clause in English? You might think there are millions, but in fact there are quite a small number. Take the clause *John saw Jim*. This has three elements, in this case each consisting of one word. But you can't put these elements into any old order, and end up with a normal English sentence. You can't have **Saw John Jim* or **Jim John saw*. Nor can you leave an element out and say **John Jim*. So, how many possible patterns of elements *are* there? In fact, there are only seven main patterns, and just a few exceptions. Here they are:

● You can have a clause with two elements, such as *John laughed*. *John* is called the **subject** and *laughed* is called the **verb**.
● You can have a clause with three elements, such as *John saw Jim*. Here, as well as the subject (*John*) and the verb (*saw*), there's an **object** (*Jim*).
● There's another type of clause with three elements, such as *John went yesterday*. Here, as well as the subject (*John*) and the verb (*went*), there's an **adverbial** (*yesterday*).
● And there's yet another type of clause with three elements, such as *John is posh*. This time, as well as the subject (*John*) and the verb (*is*) we have a **complement** (*posh*).
● Next, you can have a clause with four elements, such as *John saw Jim yesterday*. Perhaps you can work out what the elements are, as they've all been mentioned? Here goes. *John* is the subject, *saw* is the verb, *Jim* is the object, and *yesterday* is the adverbial.

- The same applies to this next type of clause, which also has four familiar elements: *John made Jim posh*. Here, *John* is the subject, *made* is the verb, *Jim* is the object, and *posh* is the complement.
- And, lastly, there's a type of clause which has two objects, as in *John gave Jim flu*. Here, *John* is the subject, *gave* is the verb, *Jim* is one object and *flu* is the other object (see the entry on **direct object**, to see the difference between the two types).

You must make sure you understand what is meant by the terms subject, verb, object, complement, and adverbial, otherwise you won't be able to analyse clauses properly, and that would be worse than giving up sweets for a year!

By the way, I've shown the seven types of clause using very simple examples, with just one word per clause element. In longer clauses, each element will have more than one word. But the basic analysis is just the same. So, *John saw Jim yesterday* is analysed in the same way as *The big dog was chasing the fat cat in the morning*. Can you see where the boundary lines are between the different elements?

clause; sentence   adverbial; complement; object; subject; verb

cleft sentence; existential sentence

cliche (**klee**-shay)

Once, in a radio programme, I gave the listeners a competition: write a sentence with as many cliches in it as possible. Here's part of the winning sentence. (I can't quote it all, because it went on for over two pages!) Oh, and don't try to follow what the sentence means – you won't succeed!

In the final analysis, I personally find myself in an ongoing situation where to be perfectly frank and honest we have to ask ourselves, at the end of the day, when all is said and done, what is it all about, for whether we like it or not, in this day and age it's as plain as the nose on your face that Rome wasn't built in a day, as every Tom Dick and Harry knows . . .

Bower is at the wicket...He must basically ask himself in all honesty, in this day & age, whether he likes it or not, for it's as plain as the nose on your face, when all's said & d.... He's out!!

You should by now be getting a good idea of what a **cliche** is: it's an expression that's been worn out by overuse. It no longer carries very much meaning. If you think about it, the three phrases *in the final analysis*, *when all is said and done*, and *at the end of the day* all mean more or less the same thing! Cliches make a lot of noise, but when you analyse the content of the noise, you won't find much there. It's wise to avoid them, then, if you want to appear clear and precise.

But cliches aren't always bad. Sometimes they can be very useful. Strangers who meet on a train, for instance, often greet each other, just to be polite. If they then don't want to start a conversation, they can simply swop a few cliches, and lapse into silence. The weather is an excellent source of cliches in English. *Turned out nice again. It's going to be another beautiful day. Yes, but the weather forecast wasn't too promising. Rain later*.

GOVERNMENT WORD WARNING! Some people spell **cliché** with an accent, like that, to remind readers how the word is pronounced. It was originally a French word, you see, and the accent was an important part of the spelling in that language. But accents aren't a normal feature of English (see the entry on **alphabet** for more on this), and these days people tend to write the word without an accent.

accent; alphabet; circumlocution; euphemism; idiom

clipping

After my exam, I met my prof in a pub (a very nice gent) and he showed me a photo of a demo he'd been to. I couldn't go 'cos I had flu, so I stayed by the phone eating fries and watching ads on the telly.

This is a very colloquial way of talking, isn't it. Why? The main reason is that several of the words (12, in fact) have been shortened. *Exam* is short for 'examination', *prof* for 'professor', *flu* for 'influenza', and so on. Words which have been shortened in this way are often called **clippings**. They're one kind of abbreviation. Can you identify the long forms of the other nine?

 abbreviation  colloquial speech

coinage see neologism

colloquial speech (kuh-**loh**-kwee-uhl)

Imagine you're on your way home from school, talking to some friends. How would you describe the kind of language you'd be using? It goes by many names, such as **casual** or **informal** or **conversational** or **everyday**, but **colloquial** is probably the one that's most widely used. It's the kind of speech you use when you're most at your ease – with your friends and family, in particular. It's definitely *not* the kind of speech you use when you feel you're on your best behaviour, and having to take care about your language. Colloquial speech is very different from the more formal speaking styles. It has its own vocabulary (e.g. *mates*, *bolshy*), its own norms of pronunciation (e.g. *gimme* instead of *give me*), and

its own grammatical rules (e.g. *Who'd you give it to?* instead of *To whom did you give it?*). Colloquial speech is the commonest of all speech styles. If someone tape-recorded everything you said from the moment you learned to speak until now, over 90 per cent of it would be colloquial. It's a carefree speech style, and nobody minds if you don't take special care with your words, sounds, and sentences. But beware! If you use this kind of speech on special occasions, such as at an interview, you may find it criticised. People expect more care on these occasions. And be very sure of your audience before you use it in writing. It's fine in a letter to a friend, but hardly appropriate in a history essay or a science report.

 audience; clipping; formal; idiom; slang; style

colon (**koh**-luhn)

There is one important thing I want to say about the **colon**: it's a type of punctuation mark formed by two dots, one on top of the other, and I've just used one. What is it for, exactly? Its main job is to separate two parts of a sentence, and to tell you that the two parts are related in a special way. The part after the colon *expands* or *explains* the part before the colon. Somebody once said that the colon is like a pair of car headlights, pointing ahead. Look at my first sentence again. The part before the colon says 'I'm going to tell you something important' – but I don't actually say what it is. The part after the colon explains what I'm talking about. (If you look at the entry on **cliche**, you'll find a good example of the colon being used as part of a definition; and there's another example coming up just after these brackets.) Another point: in careful written English, you can have only one colon per sentence. And one more thing: after the colon, it isn't usual in British English to use a capital letter – but there are a few exceptions, such as when the next sentence is quoting what someone said. *I asked Fred: What on earth is going on?*

 punctuation   semi-colon

comma (**ko**-muh)

Try reading this:

I'd like some cheese a pound of bacon sandwiches fresh fruit and matches please.

It isn't easy, is it. What's happened? All the commas have been left out. The sentence *should* have been written like this:

I'd like some cheese, a pound of bacon, sandwiches, fresh fruit, and matches, please.

Without commas, written English becomes very difficult to read. And sometimes it's impossible to make sense of what is written. Look at that first sentence again. Did you read it as 'a pound of bacon sandwiches'? And what might 'fresh matches' be? (It does say 'fresh fruit and matches'!) You can see from this example how important the **comma** is. In shape, it's very simple – it's usually printed just like a full stop with a tail (,) though in this book the designer has used a simplified form (,). It's the commonest punctuation mark of all. But it isn't easy to sum up how to use it. It has more uses than any other punctuation mark. Not only does it separate lists of nouns, as in the sentence at the beginning of the entry, it also separates lists of clauses and phrases, as in the present sentence. I've just had to use three commas to keep my sentence clear. Try writing it out without the commas, then give it to a friend to read, and you'll see how difficult it is.

Sometimes, there are clear rules about where a comma should go and where it shouldn't go. We write *One, two, three . . .* and we don't write **I have, been counting*. But there are no simple rules about using commas. For instance, don't fall into the trap of thinking that whenever there's a pause in speech you should have a comma in writing. This doesn't work. If I say, *That man sitting over there in the armchair is drunk as a lord*, I might well pause in speech after the word *armchair* – but you don't put a comma there in writing. Also, remember that in several cases there are no hard and fast rules about using commas. Some people write *The tall, dark, and dangerous house frightened me*; others write *The tall, dark and dangerous house frightened me*. I always put a comma in before *and* in such cases; but not everyone likes to do this. People have different preferences. Some people like to pepper their work with commas. Others use them as if they were gold dust. If you have your homework marked by a teacher with a liking for commas, you'll get your essay back covered in blue or red measles. And if you have it marked by a teacher who hates commas, you might find that some of your commas have been crossed out – blue or red measles again. That's life, I'm afraid. I've just had a typescript of a book returned to me by the editor of a publishing firm, and lots of my commas have been crossed out. Shame. I like commas. That publisher doesn't. We shall have a row about it next week, and I hope I win!

H punctuation   *□* inverted commas; semi-colon

command

Sit!   Stay!   Be quiet!   Get down!   Stop eating my slippers!

Jill is talking to Jack, who is, of course, her husband – sorry, I mean dog. She is giving him instructions. Sentences which do this are called **commands** or **directives**. To give a command, you use the basic form of the verb, without any endings. In writing, the sentence often finishes with an exclamation mark. You sometimes find the subject of the command mentioned: *You sit down!*, *Everybody come inside!*, *All you men in the front row, shut up!* And one other thing: you can give a command to yourself, as well as to other people. To do this, you have to use the word *let*. Let me see, now. Can I think of an example? Let's use that one.

 sentence; verb    exclamation; question; statement

common noun see **noun**

communication

1 Hello, red leader. Hello, red leader. I am right behind you. I repeat. I am right behind you. Over.
2 Fred, have I ever told you that your green hair doesn't suit you?
3 Hey! Geroff!
4 This is the six o'clock news.
5 I love you.
6 Ssshh!

These are a few examples of one person talking to another person, or to a group of people. Let's call the speaker 'A' and the listener(s) 'B'. Now, what if A couldn't speak, or if B couldn't hear? There are several other possible ways of getting a message across. A might write a message to B. This wouldn't be so easy in the case of **1**, where the two people are in different aeroplanes. It would also be highly unlikely in cases **3** and **6**. But it's common enough in cases **2** and **5**, which might be found in a letter, and even case **4** could appear in written form – in subtitles on TV, for instance. An alternative would be not to use words at all to get the message across. You could use **body language** (more technically known as **nonverbal communication**). For instance, if you're playing a game where stealth is crucial, you can signal the need for silence by putting your finger to your lips. You can tell someone you love them

by giving them a big smacking kiss. You can tell someone to 'geroff' by digging them in the ribs (or worse). If you're musical, you can sing your love to someone – pop singers are doing this all the time. And if you're artistic, you can draw or paint your message – remember X marking the spot on old treasure maps?

It's handy to have one word for *all* these different ways of sending and receiving messages – and that word is **communication**. Humans usually communicate using their senses of sound, vision, and touch – either separately, or at the same time. If someone grabbed you, as in case **3**, I can imagine you'd yell, grimace, and thump all at once! Sometimes, our senses of smell and taste are used in communication – such as when the smell of bacon cooking tells us it's breakfast-time, or you taste a substance to see what it might be. Certain animals communicate by smell and taste all the time. Humans use sound (speech, noises) and vision (writing, gestures, facial expressions) more than anything else. And language, the subject of this book, is the chief form of human communication.

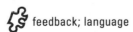 feedback; language

comparative (kuhm-**pa**-ruh-tiv)

Buy new improved Bloggo! It's bigger, cleaner, whiter, softer! It's more delicious, more fascinating, more comfortable than ever before! It's less dirty, less smelly. You'll be able to use it more quickly, more reliably, more . . .

That's enough. If you don't know what a **comparative** is now, you never will. In some cases, as you can see, it's a special form of a word. When you add *-er* onto an adjective, you can use it to make a comparison, as with *bigger* and the others. In the other cases, you make the comparison by putting *more* or *less* in front of the adjective or adverb that's being compared. If you want, what you're comparing can be expressed in full by using a **comparative clause**, beginning with the word *than*. *Agatha is taller – than Jemima? than she was a month ago? than other children of her age? than a rotweiler?* Until you know what Agatha is being compared with, you can't really make much sense of the sentence. So, beware advertisements which tell you 'Our new product is cheaper'. You want to ask: 'Cheaper than what?'

 adjective; adverb; clause   degree; superlative

complement (**kom**-pli-muhnt)

Erica saw a doctor.
Erica is a doctor.

What's the difference between these two sentences? Obvious, I suppose. In the first sentence, Erica and the doctor are different people. In the second sentence, they're the same person. When we're naming the parts of a sentence, we call *a doctor* in the first sentence the **object** of the verb *saw* (see the entry on **object** for more information). What shall we call *a doctor* in the second sentence? We need a term which gives us the idea that *Erica* and *a doctor* are two ways of talking about the same thing. Well, the term that the grammar-book writers have cooked up for us is **complement**. Do you know this word at all (spelled with an *e* in the middle)? If I say *The ship has its full complement of officers and men*, I mean it has everyone on board – the numbers are complete. Similarly, in grammar, a complement 'completes' the meaning of another part of the sentence. In the above example, it completes the

meaning of the subject of the sentence. *Erica is –* Wait for it! *– a doctor.* Whew! Now we know. So, let's have some other examples of complements:

Horatio's car is *a Porsche*.
Horatio and Horace are *happy*.

Notice the importance of *is* and *are*, and other forms of the verb *be*, in these examples. They help to show the identity between the subject and the complement.

There's one other kind of complement you should know about, by the way. Look at this sentence:

John called Jim an idiot.

Who's the idiot? John or Jim? Jim, of course. So what we have here is *an idiot* completing the meaning of *Jim*. It's another kind of complement – a complement to the object, this time.

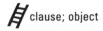 clause; object

compound word

One of the remarkable things about English is the way you can make new words by putting old words together. You know *black*. You know *bird*. And you know *blackbird*. When you get words like this, they're called **compound words** – or **compounds**, for short. There are hundreds of thousands of compounds in English, especially in science. Here's a short list taken from everyday usage:

Anglo-French	daydream	home-made	sleepwalker
chewing-gum	firing squad	motorcycle	table leg
crybaby	gold mine	scarecrow	waiting room
dance hall	headache	sea-green	washing-machine

Have you noticed something? Compound words are sometimes written without any space between the elements; sometimes there's a hyphen; and sometimes there's a space. With a word like *flowerpot*, you'll find that usage varies a lot, with some people writing

Honey bee... Sugar plum... Cherry blossom... Pussy cat...

Half wit!

flowerpot, some *flower-pot*, and some *flower pot*. So, don't be fooled by the space. Just because there's a space between two words doesn't prove anything. You must check to see whether the two elements on either side of the space make up a compound word or not. How do you check? Well, do the two words make up a single meaning? And do they stick together, grammatically? Let's try this out. *Motorcycle* isn't just a 'motor' and a 'cycle' – it's a special kind of vehicle. And you have to say *new motorcycle* and *expensive motorcycle*:

you can't split the two parts and say *motor new cycle* or *motor expensive cycle*. *Motorcycle* is definitely a compound. Try out this kind of check on some of the other words.

 hyphen; word  morphology

concord (**kon**-kawd)

No, this isn't the name of an aeroplane. Apart from anything else, the name of the aeroplane ends with an *e*: *Concorde*. **Concord**, without the *e*, is something you have to have when you're building up a sentence in English. The term basically means 'agreement' or 'harmony'. If you're in concord with people, you agree with them. It's the same with grammar. To make an acceptable sentence, certain words have to **agree**. To understand how it works, fill the blank in these three sentences with a word ending in *-self*.

I hurt –. He hurt –. She hurt –.

Can you see what's happening? You had to put *myself* in the first sentence, *himself* in the second, and *herself* in the third. You can't say **I hurt himself* or **She hurt myself*. Why not? Because it's a rule of English grammar that the *-self* word (it's called a **reflexive pronoun**) has to agree with the subject of the sentence.

Sometimes you can have several words agreeing with each other in the same sentence. Look at these two:

That TV is expensive. Those TVs are expensive.
This bike is a beauty. These bikes are beauties.

The point is, you can't have any other combination. You can't say:

*That TV are expensive. *This bikes is a beauties.

That's what concord is all about.

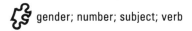 gender; number; subject; verb

conjunction (kon-**junk**-shuhn)

TEACHER: This homework is awful, Smith!
SMITH: But –
TEACHER: I can't read most of it!
SMITH: But –

TEACHER: Most of the bits I *can* read don't make sense!
SMITH: But –
TEACHER: And the bits that do make sense are wrong!
SMITH: But –
TEACHER: Only an idiot would think you'd spent time on it!
SMITH: But –
TEACHER: Do I look like an idiot, Smith?
SMITH: But –
TEACHER: Why do you keep butting in, Smith?
SMITH: Because that's not my homework, sir.

Poor old Smith! He couldn't get a word in edgeways. Or rather, he did get *one* word in, but it didn't get him very far. All he could do was show that he wanted to say something, linked to what had just been said – and also, that he wanted to disagree. *But* did the job. It's one of the linking words, or **conjunctions**, in English. It's not the most frequently used conjunction, though. That prize goes to *and*, which is one of the commonest words in the language.

So why use conjunctions at all? Compare these two stories, and you'll see:

The train stopped suddenly. My bag fell off the rack.
The train stopped suddenly, and my bag fell off the rack.

What's the difference? The *and* turns two sentences into one, and as a result the *meanings* of the two sentences become linked. You feel: the train stopped, and *therefore* the bag fell off the rack. A conjunction isn't just an extra word; it's an extra meaning as well.

There are two kinds of conjunction. The ones which just 'join together' (or **coordinate**) words, phrases, and sentences are called **coordinating conjunctions**, or **coordinators**. The chief ones are *and*, *or*, and *but*. The other conjunctions are called **subordinating conjunctions**, or **subordinators**. Their job is to show that one clause is *part* of another clause. They include *when, because, if, although, since,* and *while*. There are over 50 altogether, expressing several kinds of meaning. Here's an example of some subordinating conjunctions doing their job. Notice how the meaning changes, although the linked sentences stay the same:

Florence went to town *because* Fred went to work.
Florence went to town *before* Fred went to work.
Florence went to town *until* Fred went to work.

 parts of speech    connectivity; coordination; subordination

connectivity

Here's a game you can play at parties, if you've got nothing better to do. I call it 'connections'. Each person takes a slip of paper, and secretly writes a silly sentence about one of the people in the room. You fold the pieces of paper so that no one can see what's written. Then divide the pieces of paper into two equal piles. Next, make a third pile with linking words such as *and*, *because*, *when*, *after*, and *although* (see the entry on **conjunction** for some other examples). The game is to choose one sentence from the first pile; then a linking word; then a sentence from the second pile. If you're lucky, you can get some brilliant results. Here are some I've seen:

First sentence	Linking word	Second sentence
Mary was sick on the bus	because	John's got a large nose.
Mike saw Meg in a red dress	and	We all want to go to the toilet.
Trudy wants to go to the moon	after	Fred's bought a new pair of socks.

You can try the same game using other words and phrases (**adverbials**) to link the sentences, such as *fortunately*, *three weeks later*, and *so*. Try them in the above sequences, and see what happens.

In language, we make connections like this all the time, without realising it. We don't speak or write in single sentences. One sentence links with another. Sometimes you string your own sentences together – such as when you're telling a story or a joke. Sometimes you link a sentence with the one someone else has just said – such as in a conversation. And there are other ways of showing **connectivity** between sentences, apart from using linking words and phrases such as those shown above. Look at this pair of sentences, for example:

Christopher bought Belinda a parrot. He got it for her on Wednesday.

You can see how the words in the second sentence depend for their meaning on the words in the first sentence. *He* refers back to *Christopher*; *it* refers to *parrot*; and *her* refers to *Belinda*. It wouldn't make sense to have these sentences the other way round. Try it and see!

 sentence    adverbial; conjunction; pronoun    coherence; cohesion

continuous see **progressive**

contraction

Here's Jennie. She won't be pleased.
You're right. I'm off. Let's go.

That's how people talk in real life. They
don't usually say:

Here is Jennie. She will not be pleased.
You are right. I am off. Let us go.

They shorten the verbs, and this gives an
informal or colloquial tone to their speech.
The shortened form of a word is called a
contraction. Not many words can be
contracted in English – just a few verbs
(some of the auxiliary verbs, in fact), and a
few other words, such as *not* (*n't*) and *us*
(in *let's*). Because contractions are a sure
sign of colloquial speech, it's unusual to
see them in the written language – unless
the writer is aiming to be informal, of
course, or is writing down a conversation.
I don't think you'll find many reference
books at secondary level which use
contractions, unless they're deliberately
adopting a chatty tone – like this one!

🪜 apostrophe; colloquial speech

🧩 auxiliary verb; verb

Hello – I am Polly. I am a very clever but rather formal parrot. I do hope I am not getting on your nerves. Who is a pretty boy then? I expect you will be putting the cover on my cage soon....

conversation

Everybody knows what a **conversation** is, so why have an entry on
it in a language book? I suppose the main reason is to remind you of
how important it is. It's the normal way of behaving, when you use
spoken language. Everything else is special, and you have to learn
how to do it – making a speech, taking part in a debate, saying a
prayer, giving a report . . . But conversation just seems to come
naturally.

In fact, when you investigate what a conversation is, and how it
works, you find all kinds of rules – and if you don't follow these

rules, the conversation is a disaster. Imagine a conversation where one person does all the talking and nobody else gets a look in. You may know someone a bit like that – it's not much of a conversation, is it! To be a good conversation, everybody taking part must have a chance to say something. Listen out, too, to the way people start a conversation, and how they finish it off. Here's a list of things people say. See if you can work out which would go at the beginning and which would go at the end.

Lovely day!
Good heavens, is that the time?
Excuse me, have you got a match?
I mustn't keep you.
Nice talking to you.
Sorry to trouble you, but . . .
Can I help you?
Must get back to work, I suppose.
Did you hear the one about the . . .

And here's a list of some of the things people say when they're in the middle of a conversation and they want to change the topic:

That reminds me . . .
By the way . . .
Incidentally . . .
Talking about that . . .

These are just a few of the things we all do, without thinking, whenever we get into a conversation. And that means dozens of times, every day, for the rest of our lives.

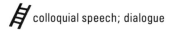 colloquial speech; dialogue   text

conversion (kuhn-**ver**-shuhn)

Right, class, what part of speech is *round*? Did you say adjective? Give me an example. *A round table.* Good. End of story? No. Because I heard someone else say adverb – as in *We turned round*. She was right, too. And the person who said preposition was also right – as in *round the corner*. I also have a feeling that the more sporty of you were thinking it's a verb – as in *The yacht is about to round the breakwater*. Correct. And I distinctly heard some drunkard at the back say it was a noun – as in *It's your round*! In fact, everyone's

...so I set out to set him a hard set to win. He was dead set on being set fair until an early set-back set me on the way. In the third set we were all set for a real set-to but I set about him and that set me up for the final set......

I was set against doing this interview right from the outset...

right. *Round* has as many as five different uses in English. It can act as five different parts of speech.

It's very common for a word to move like that from one use to another. It's an important way of making up new words without having to add any extra bits on at the beginning or at the end (see the entry on **affix**, to find out about this other way of making up new words). A word which starts off life as a noun may very well turn into a verb. Or a noun might become an adjective. Or the other way round. When a word changes its use in this way, we call it **conversion**. Here are some other examples of words which have been converted from one part of speech into another:

I'd like a *swim*.	I'd like to *swim*.
I'm reading a *paper*.	I'm about to *paper* the lounge.
This is the *final* episode.	He's going to see the *final*.
Pass the *butter*.	You *butter* the bread.
Hand me one over.	Look at my *hand*.

You can experiment with words to see how conversion works. Take a noun and see if you can make a verb out of it. A telephone? To telephone. A book? To book. A tree? To tree.

To tree? Sorry! Just trying to catch you out.

adjective; adverb; affix; noun; parts of speech; preposition; verb; word

coordination (koh-aw-di-**nay**-shuhn)

Janet	and	John
a cat	and	a dog
a big fat cat	and	a small thin dog
walking in the rain	and	running in the snow
Mr Jones travelled by train	and	Mrs Jones travelled by bus

What's going on here? In each case, two bits of language are being linked by the word *and*. Have you noticed how similar these bits are? They have the same sort of pattern and the same sort of meaning. You can even have the bits the other way round, if you want. Try it. *John and Janet. A dog and a cat.* No problem. Also, you can carry on adding a further bit linked by *and* for as long as you like:

Janet and John and Steven and Ben and Lucy and Susan and Rebecca and Alexander . . .

It gets boring, but it's allowed! Constructions of this kind are examples of **coordination**, and the linking word is called a **coordinating conjunction**, or **coordinator**. There are three main coordinators in English: *and*, *or*, and *but*. To see how *or* works, you can just replace *and* by *or* in the above list. *But* is rather different, as you have to find examples which make a nice contrast in meaning, such as *The weather will be fine but windy* or *Hilary got an invitation but she didn't want to go.*

46

Before I forget: with coordination you can often leave out part of one construction, because you can read in that bit of meaning from the other. Look at these:

Mr Jones flew to New York and he drove to Washington.
Mr Jones flew to New York and drove to Washington.

You don't need to say *he*; it's obvious who it is. These are examples of coordination, too, but this time you can't swop the bits around. Try it. *Drove to Washington and Mr Jones flew to New York*. No way. And beware the cases where, if you swop the bits around, you get a new meaning. Is *John died and was buried* the same as *John was buried and died*? I don't think so, somehow.

 conjunction; subordination

correctness

2 + 2 = 4? Correct.   2 + 2 = 5? Incorrect.

That's what correctness normally means, isn't it. The answer is right or wrong. There are no two ways about it. 'Do your corrections' means 'Get it right next time – or else!' When we talk about **correctness** in English, it means we are following the rules of the language. Little children who say *Me not like dem mouses* aren't speaking English correctly, because they've not learned all the rules yet. So what are these rules? They're rules which say how we use words, how we join words together to make sentences, how we pronounce words, and how we spell them. So, *That goldfish looks seasick* is correct grammar, *Goldfish that seasick looks* isn't. *Goldfish* is the correct spelling; *golfish* isn't. And if you pronounced *goldfish* as 'goshfish', that wouldn't be correct either.

When everybody uses the language in the same way, it's easy to talk about usage being 'correct' or 'incorrect'. The trouble is, there are lots of cases in English when people *don't* use the language in the same way. Think about these:

● Some people spell the word *judgement* with an *e* in the middle; some don't – *judgment*.
● Some people pronounce the word *envelope* so that the *en-* rhymes with *hen*; some make the *en-* rhyme with *on*. (Which pronunciation do you and your friends use? Be prepared to find some differences.)
● Some people say *X is different from Y*; some say *X is different to Y*; some say *X is different than Y*. (Which is the construction you and your friends normally use? Again, be prepared to find differences.)

When usage varies in this way, people often feel that one of the alternatives is better than the other(s), and they call this the 'correct' usage, and the other(s) 'incorrect'. 'Onvelope', they say, 'is the correct way to pronounce that word.' Of course, this then upsets the people who *don't* pronounce *envelope* in this way – and there are millions of them. So, when lots of people favour one usage, and lots of people favour another, it's a bit difficult to talk about 'correctness' at all. Instead, linguists try to discover the reasons for the difference. Perhaps people from the south prefer one usage, and people from the north prefer another? Perhaps older people prefer one usage, and younger people another? Or perhaps the difference is to do with where you were educated, or the kind of social occasion it is, or the sort of job you have, or whether you're male or female? In such cases, it's better not to talk about one usage being 'correct' and the other being 'incorrect'; rather, say that one usage is 'appropriate' in one set of circumstances, and 'inappropriate' in another.

 usage   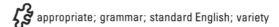 appropriate; grammar; standard English; variety

dash

You are writing the last episode of your latest TV play, 'The Horror from the Black Pit'. Cathy, your heroine, looks out of the window and sees the monster coming towards the house. She tries to tell the others, but she's so scared that she can't get the words out. She keeps starting her sentences but can't finish them. How will you write down what she says? This is where you'll find the **dash** a particularly useful punctuation mark.

CATHY: Look! It's – It's –
MARION: What is it, Cathy?
CATHY: There's a – There's a –
MIKE: Cathy, what can you see?!

If it goes on like this, of course, there'll soon be an 'Aaaargh' to finish things off. These examples show you what the main job of the dash is: it marks a break in a sentence. The break might be caused by someone being interrupted, or breaking down, or being forgetful – or it might simply be an extra point, tacked on to the main sentence (as here). You'll also find the dash being used in order to replace letters in a word, or to show a missing word in a sentence. Crossword puzzle clues often do this: 'Romeo, Romeo, wherefore art —, Romeo' (4 letters). And if you want an example of the dash replacing letters in a word, keep an eye open in novels where people are doing some swearing. You may find items like b– – – –y, for instance. You'll gather from this that the dash is generally found only in the more informal varieties of written English!

 punctuation

48

definite article see **article**

degree

JULIE: It was a hot day yesterday. The temperature reached 25° in the afternoon.
KYLIE: Yes, but it'll be hotter today – might be as high as 27° or 28°.
JULIE: Still, I wish I was in Spain. Where Alec's staying was the hottest spot in Europe last week – well over 30°.

The ° symbol stands for 'degrees', and as you can see from the examples, the more degrees you have, the hotter it is. Elementary physics. The same basic idea is found in language. Here, variations in the range or intensity of something are called differences of **degree**. They're expressed using a type of adverb – **adverbs of degree**. You can put these degree words on a scale, if you like, as with temperature, going from the highest degree possible to the lowest degree possible. Can you see the scale of 'greenness' in these phrases?

HIGH END	*completely green*	–	*very green*	–	*rather green*	–	*hardly green*	LOW END

Other common degree words are *quite, a bit, somewhat, more, most, extremely,* and *scarcely.* Can you feel which are the 'high degree' words and which are the 'low degree' words in this list?

Differences of degree are especially important when you're comparing adjectives and adverbs. Start with an adjective, such as *hot* or *interesting.* Now, compare these words to a *higher* degree. You can do this, first of all, by using the *-er* ending or the word *more,* and this is called the **comparative** form. *Hot, hotter. Interesting, more interesting.* You can then compare them to an even higher degree, by using the *-est* ending or the word *most,* and this is called the **superlative** form. *Hot, hotter, hottest. Interesting, more interesting, most interesting.* If you want to go the other way, and compare them to a *lower* degree, you can do this using *less* and *least. Less hot, least hot. Less interesting, least interesting.* And if you want to say that something is there in the *same* degree, you can do this by using the word *as* twice – like this: *Madrid is as hot as Nice, Mary is as interesting as Jane.*

Do grammar books have a name for an adjective or adverb when it isn't being compared at all? Do cats chase mice? Does chocolate melt in the sun? Grammarians can't get to sleep at night if they haven't thought up a name for something. When words like *hot* and *interesting* are used on their own, they're said to be in the **positive** or **absolute** degree. There you are, *two* names. Value for money, eh?

 adjective; adverb   comparative; superlative

dependent clause see subordination

derivation (de-ri-**vay**-shuhn)

Roll up! Roll up! Pick a word. Any word! All right – *camera.* Now, tell me where it comes from. What is its history? If you look it up in a dictionary which tells you about the history of words, you'll find that it's a long story. In ancient Greek, the word meant any area with an arched cover. In Latin, it meant an arched roof or chamber.

English borrowed the word in this sense, and in the eighteenth century it was used in the phrase *camera obscura* (this is Latin for 'dark room'). A camera obscura is a darkened room into which light passes through a small hole, reflecting the images of outside objects onto a surface in the room. A small box did the same kind of thing, and this led to the way the word *camera* is used today. So, the history, or **derivation**, of this word goes back over 2,000 years.

The derivation of a word, then, is the whole story of where that word comes from (or **derives**), as far as we know. And you can use the same term to talk about the words we make up today, especially when we invent a new word by adding bits to an old word. *Goodness* derives from the joining together of *good* and *-ness*. *Brunch* derives from *breakfast* and *lunch*. 'What's the derivation of *brunch*?', someone might ask. Well, now you know.

 affix; borrowing; etymology

dialect (**die**-uh-lekt)

Where's this person from? 'Hey, y'all, whose automobile is parked on the sidewalk?' And this person? 'Hey, Jimmy, d'you no see the wee lassie waving at you?' And this one? 'Hey there, wack, who's that gear judy in the jigger?'

Did you get the USA, Scotland, and Liverpool? Even if you didn't, I'm sure you were able to see that the three sentences were showing the different ways people speak, depending on which part of the world they come from. Certain words and phrases give the game away. *Automobile* and *sidewalk* are American English; in Britain we'd say *car* and *pavement*. For *y'all* (= 'you all') we'd probably say *everyone* or *everybody*. In the Scots example, you'll have noticed *wee* (= 'little') and *lassie* ('girl'), and the use of *no* (= 'not'). In the Liverpool example,

there's *gear* (great), *judy* (girl), *jigger* (back alley), and *wack* (mate). These are all features of **dialect** – they tell you where someone comes from. Usually, when people talk about dialects, they mean **regional dialects**: showing a person's geographical origins in a particular country or locality or city. International dialects of English include British, American, Indian, Australian, and South African. Within Britain, we have Welsh, Scots, and Irish English, plus the dialects of immigrant groups, such as Jamaican English. Many parts of the country have their own dialects, such as Yorkshire, Lancashire, and the West Country. And some cities have their own dialects, too, such as Liverpool (Scouse), Birmingham (Brummie), and London (Cockney).

Keep your ears open for other kinds of dialect, apart from the regional ones. Some dialects will tell you where the speakers are from socially. Do they sound as if they've been educated in a public school, for instance? These are called **social dialects** or **class dialects**. The main social dialect that *you've* already learned belongs to the written language – the kind of educated writing that you're reading now. (See the entry on **standard English** to find out more about it.) You'll also hear people talking about **occupational dialects** – varieties of the language which tell you the sort of job a person does (speaking like a lawyer, or a priest, or a scientist, for instance).

GOVERNMENT WORD WARNING! Don't mix up a dialect and an **accent**. You recognise a dialect because of its distinctive words and constructions. An accent is solely a matter of pronunciation. People in both Glasgow and Edinburgh speak the Scots dialect of English, but their accents are very different. And many kinds of accents are used when people speak standard English.

accent; standard English; variety

idiolect; pidgin

dialogue (**die**-uh-log) and monologue (**mon**-uh-log)

I thought you'd like to read the beginning of my latest play. It's all about Robin Hood.

ROBIN: Hello, Little John.
JOHN: Hello, Robin.
ROBIN: How are you, today?
JOHN: Fine, thanks.

Not bad, eh? A fantastic success, I'm sure you'll be saying. (I heard that! Who said 'rubbish'?) Well, even if it's a flop, at least I've given you an example of a **dialogue** – an exchange of language between

two people. Usually, a dialogue is a spoken conversation, but of course it could be written down, as in a play script, or when two governments formally 'talk' to each other by sending letters. So, what's a **monologue**, then? It's when only *one* person does all the talking. *Mono-* means 'one' as in *monorail* (one railway line) and *monoplane* (one set of wings). Can you think of occasions when just one person talks, and you have to listen, without even being able to interrupt? I'll start you off: a sermon, a speech, the person reading the news on the radio, a judge summing up in court – and the headteacher at morning assembly.

You can sometimes find stretches of monologue *within* a dialogue. Watch what happens next time you're having a conversation (a dialogue) and someone says: 'Hey, do you know the one about the Englishman, the Irishman, the Scotsman, and the hairy underpants?' From that point on, it's a monologue. You're not allowed to interrupt or change the subject until the joke is over – unless you decide to be rude, of course. And if it looks like being a really rotten joke, you might well want to be!

 conversation   discourse

diction (**dik**-shuhn)

TEACHER: Now, describe the picture.
DAVID: Well, it's nice, Miss.
TEACHER: What precisely is nice about it, David?
DAVID: It's got some nice things in it, Miss.
TEACHER: Can you be more specific?
DAVID: There are two nice things in it, Miss.

I think that'll do for now. David seems to have a pretty pathetic range of vocabulary, doesn't he? He chooses the same words each time, and they don't mean very much. The teacher's doing rather better, wouldn't you say, with *describe*, *precisely*, and *specific*? (Yes, all right, I'm a creep.) When we study how well people have chosen their words, we talk about **diction**. How clear are the words? How effective are they in painting a picture? How good are they at persuading you to do something? Some words are vague, some are sharp, some are vivid; some growl at you, some purr at you. Paying attention to your diction can make all the difference between an interesting and a boring conversation, or a good and a bad piece of writing.

 vocabulary

dictionary

DAUGHTER: Dad, it says in the paper, 'The soldiers yomped across the desert'. What does 'yomped' mean?
DAD: I'm busy. Look it up in the dictionary!

I imagine you've had a conversation like this, from time to time. So, I hope you've got a good dictionary. If you haven't, get it on your next Christmas or birthday list right now. When you get it, don't let anybody borrow it. And remember where you put it. (In one house I know, the dictionary is holding up a wonky fridge!) A **dictionary** gives you information about words – in alphabetical order, from A to Z – especially how they're spelled and pronounced, what they mean, and how they're used. Some dictionaries give you all kinds of other goodies, too, such as where the words come from originally (the **etymology**), and essays on how certain words should be used. There's only one slight problem with a dictionary. To look a word up, you have to know how to spell it. If you start looking for *pneumonia* under *N* (because it's pronounced nyoo-**mohn**-yuh), you're going to have a long and fruitless search.

Dictionaries come in all sizes, from small 'pocket' dictionaries of just
a few thousand words to huge volumes of over half a million words.
To be sure you have something which includes most of the new
words and meanings you'll meet during secondary school, you
need a book of at least 50,000 words. Anything less, and it won't be
so helpful. There ought to be an even bigger dictionary in the school
library, containing the rarer words in the language. Find out where
it's kept. (And if it isn't there, you'd better persuade the Parent-
Teacher Association to put on a jumble sale to get one!)

By the way, a dictionary goes out of date quite quickly, because of
all the new words coming into the language. Some people change
their car every few years, just to keep up to date. You should get a
new edition of a dictionary every few years too.

 vocabulary   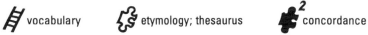 etymology; thesaurus    concordance

direct object and indirect object

When a verb takes an object, there's usually only one:

I ate *a cream bun*.   We scored *a goal*.

There are some uses in English, though, where you can have *two*
objects. Look at this sentence:

Miranda gave Marmaduke a clip on the ear.

55

Now, don't ask me what Marmaduke had been up to. Pay attention to the sentence. Miranda gave *what*? *A clip on the ear*. Who did she give it to? *Marmaduke*. When you 'give', you always have to give 'somebody something'. Or, of course, the other way round: you can give 'something to somebody'. When she'd forgiven him, Miranda might have 'given a letter to Marmaduke'. In grammar, the thing that you give is called the **direct object**, and who you give it to is the **indirect object**. Here are some other verbs that take two objects. Try them out to be sure they work both ways round.

Miss Smith teaches us English.   Miss Smith teaches English to us.

That one's OK. Now try these verbs: *pay, tell, show, see, send*.

What's that? You can't make *see* work? You're right. Sorry, I was trying to catch you out. *See* doesn't take two objects – only one.

 object; verb    transitive verb

direct speech and indirect speech

'Do you promise to tell the truth, the whole truth, and nothing but the truth?'	'I do.'	She said she did.
'Is your name Jemima Puddleduck Crystal?'	'It is.'	She said it was.
'Do you live at 1006 Riverside Lane, Crudhampton?'	'I do.'	She said she did.
Can you tell us what you saw on the night of the 16th?'	'I can.'	She said she could.

I could go on, but you've probably seen the point. There are two ways of reporting what someone says. One way, you give the exact words that were used. If you write them down, you can show that they're the real words by putting them in inverted commas. This is called **direct speech**. The second way uses a reporter, who gives an account of what was said. There aren't any inverted commas. This is called **indirect speech** or **reported speech**. All sorts of changes take place when you switch from direct to indirect speech and back again. Look carefully at these sentences:

Nadia said, 'I'm going to buy myself a compact disc player.'
Nadia said that she was going to buy herself a compact disc player.

Notice how *I* becomes *she*, *myself* becomes *herself*, and the verb *am* becomes *was*. It wouldn't be right to say:

Nadia said that I'm going to buy myself a compact disc player.

This would mean that the *reporter* was going to buy the player – whereas actually it's Nadia. You can see the problem. If you don't switch the pronouns and the verb tenses correctly, you could end up saying what you don't mean. And sometimes these changes get quite complex. Look how many words have to change in this sentence:

Maria told Tim, 'I've been waiting for you here in this cafe since early this morning.'
Maria told Tim that she'd been waiting for him there in that cafe since early that morning.

 inverted commas; pronoun; tense    free direct speech

double negative see **negative**

drafting

Take a look at the entry you're reading now. It looks very fine, doesn't it? Neat, clear (I hope), no crossing-out. Well, that's what you'd expect, in a book. But the entry didn't start out like that. It first saw the light of day, believe it or not, on a train at Llandudno Junction station. It was in very rough form – what's called a **draft**. It contained 11 crossings-out, of various sizes. The writing wobbled all over the place. When I got home, I typed up my draft, and made another dozen or so changes – some large, some small. I read it through again. Still not right. Three more changes, and I was happy. The entry said what I wanted it to say. I hadn't left anything out. (I then gave it to a few people to read, to see if they were happy too – but that's another story!)

This process of writing out a rough version of something is called **drafting**.

It's an essential feature of *all* kinds of formal writing. Everybody does it, whether the author is writing a novel, a poem, an essay, a poster, or a letter for a job. A good draft looks a real mess after you've read through it. It'll have all kinds of crossings-out, arrows reminding you to change the order of words or sentences, and tiny bits of writing crammed in between lines. Once you write (or type) it out again, it begins to look quite impressive. Some people do three or four drafts before they're happy with a letter. I wrote a poem once which went through over 400 drafts before I let it go. Of course, I'm sure you haven't got time to write your work out over and over again. But always do a rough draft of anything complex or important, in the form of notes or headings – and don't start writing properly until you're sure you've got all the ideas in, and put them in the right order. Don't think of it as a waste of time. It'll *save* you time in the end, and your work will look and read much better. In an exam, especially, always use a few minutes for drafting the structure of an answer. It'll be worth it.

 ambiguous; audience; topic sentence

etymology (e-ti-**mol**-uh-jee)

At a party the other night, the host welcomed everyone with a glass of punch. It was a cold evening. 'I wonder why they call it punch?', someone asked. The person who made the punch grinned. 'When you've tasted this, you'll find out,' he said. 'It'll knock you over!' He was right. It was powerful stuff, and for a while I forgot all about the English language. When I woke up, I remembered what I'd meant to say. It was this. That's not why punch has its name. It's nothing to do with being punched. The word is probably from Hindi, a language spoken in India, where it means 'five', and

And this is my wife, Dorothy

referred to the fact that the drink had five different ingredients. Next time he has a party, I must tell him.

Most people find the history of words absolutely fascinating. And when you search out the history of a word, you are studying its **etymology**. Here are a few other interesting etymologies. An earlier meaning of *villain* was 'farm labourer'; *sly* used to mean 'wise'; and *naughty* meant 'worth nothing'. And don't forget the etymology of people's names and place names. *Dorothy* meant 'gift of God'. *Alaska* is Eskimo for 'great land'.

 vocabulary   derivation

euphemism (**yoo**-fuh-miz-uhm)

I hear that poor old Charlie has passed on, kicked the bucket, gone over to the other side, gone to meet his maker, and snuffed the candle.

What has Charlie done? He's died, of course. All of these words and phrases are ways people use to avoid stating the plain fact. They don't like talking about death, so they 'hide' it behind a curtain of language. Phrases which talk indirectly about something unpleasant or offensive are called **euphemisms**. The three main topics which attract euphemisms are death, sex, and toileting. Listen out the next time someone says they need to go to the toilet. What do they say? I've heard 'I'm just going to wash my hands . . . powder my nose . . . pay a visit . . . find the little house . . .' I've got quite an interesting euphemism collection now. Why don't you start one?

 vocabulary   taboo word

exclamation

Gosh!   Oh no!   Help!   How awful!   Yuk!   What a mug! Marvellous!

If I asked you to read these sentences aloud, you'd know from the special kind of punctuation that they have to be read in a special tone of voice. They are all **exclamations** – sentences which express a strong emotion. No prizes for guessing what the punctuation mark is called – yes, an **exclamation mark** or **exclamation point**. This mark doesn't just show extra loudness, though. It shows that the sentence has a special meaning. You might be surprised, or shocked, or angry, or delighted, or expressing any of hundreds of emotions. Here's an example of how a sentence changes its meaning when an exclamation mark is used:

I thought the wallpaper was lovely.
I thought the wallpaper was lovely!

The first one means what it says. The second one *might* mean 'I really do think the wallpaper is lovely', but you could imagine someone saying it in a sarcastic way, meaning 'I think it's awful'. In informal writing, you can make these meanings even more intense by using extra exclamation marks. Help! No answer. Help! Still no answer. Help!!! But don't use them too much. If you scatter them everywhere in your writing, they'll lose all their force!!!!

 punctuation; sentence   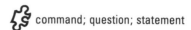 command; question; statement

feedback

Next time you're in a cafe, or just hanging about, watch what happens when two people are talking to each other. When one person talks, the other person doesn't stay silent. There's a running commentary of *m*, *yeah*, *uhuh*, and other such noises. These are important noises, as they show the speaker that the listener is paying attention. It's crucial to keep them flowing, otherwise the conversation will break down. (If you don't believe me, next time someone's talking to you, deliberately *don't* use any of these noises. The speaker will think you've gone deaf, or died, or something!) The noises send

(or feed') information back to the speaker about how you feel about what's being said, and so they're known as **feedback**. But feedback isn't purely a matter of language. The face gives feedback too – in the way you smile or frown, shake your head or nod. And don't forget your arms, your hands, and the whole way you hold your body – leaning forward in an interested way or lolling back looking bored. You can even provide some feedback in the way you smell, but as this is a polite book I won't go into that.

 communication

feminine see **gender**

60

figure of speech

John turned the air blue with his swearing.
Jane laughed like a drain.
Julie hasn't got a sausage.

She has the skin of a rhinoceros

I hope you don't think that there is really a blue colour around John, that Jane's laugh sounds like water flowing down a pipe, or that Julie is short of something to eat? If you do, you've missed the point of these expressions, which are all ways of saying something in a specially vivid or dramatic way. They're called **figures of speech**. Some figures of speech are so old and well known that they don't have much force any more. We take them for granted. Poets, on the other hand, are always looking for new figures of speech, to get their meaning across in a fresh and striking way:

The iron tongue of midnight hath told twelve . . .
Now sleeps the crimson petal, now the white . . .
As idle as a painted ship upon a painted ocean . . .

But it's not just poets who use figures of speech. Everyone does. And you can invent your own new ones, if you want. A good place to start is by making comparisons. Finish off this sentence in the most vivid way you can imagine. I'll start you off:

Fred's moustache was as small as – a full stop in the middle of a dictionary.
– a pimple on the backside of an elephant.

Your turn.

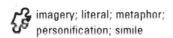 imagery; literal; metaphor; personification; simile

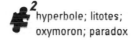 hyperbole; litotes; oxymoron; paradox

61

first language and second language

What was the language you learned to speak when you were a baby? English? Welsh? Gaelic? Hindi? Chinese? Whatever it was, you probably learned it from your mother, so it's often called your **mother tongue**. (You might have learned it from your father, of course, but nobody ever goes round talking about their *father tongue*!) It's also called your **native language** or **first language**, because – well, because it was the first language you ever learned. (Not the most helpful of sentences in this book, that one, I know – I'll try to do better in a moment.) Now, let's imagine you've been lucky, and after a while you come to learn another language really well – so well, in fact, that you come to use it often in everyday life. You've now got *two* languages, so what shall we call the difference between them? We usually call the mother tongue the **first language** and the additional language the **second language**. In many African countries, for example, the local language is the person's first language, and English or French is the person's second language. English is often used in school, in parliament, in the law courts, and on radio and TV. It's an *official* second language. But remember: to have a second language, you really have to be very fluent in it, so that you can use it quite naturally – though it'll never be as instinctive as your mother tongue, of course. If you've just learned a few irregular verbs in French or German, I'm afraid you can't say that you've got a second language yet. But if you keep working at it, in a few years' time, who knows?

 language    bilingual; fluency

fluency (**floo**-uhn-see)

BILL: How many languages are you fluent in?
BEN: Two.
BILL: Oh, which?
BEN: English and swearing.

All right. Groan. But at least it gives you an idea of what **fluency** means. If you're **fluent** in a language, you don't have to think about speaking it. The language just comes out when you want it to. You can speak it quite quickly. You're not hesitating all the time. You've got a wide range of vocabulary. You know most of the grammar. Your pronunciation has begun to sound like that of a native speaker. And you can understand most of what is said to you. You may not be perfect, but you're good!

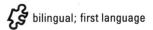 bilingual; first language

formal and informal

A That's the chap I lent my Walkman to.
B That is the gentleman to whom I loaned my Walkman.

A I would've asked, only my mum said not to.
B I would have asked, save that my mother advised I should not.

How are these pairs of sentences different? In each case, the first sounds everyday, casual, natural; the second sounds extremely careful, as if you're on your very best behaviour. In a word, the first set is **informal** language, the second set is **formal** language. If you want to be fluent in English, you have to learn about both of these styles. Being informal comes naturally, of course. You learn that at your mother's knee. It's the formal style which is more difficult. You learn that partly at home, partly in special situations (such as in church), and partly in school – especially when you learn to write.

I say there— Aren't you the gentleman who reversed his motor car into the rear of mine causing extensive damage to my rear lights before procee- —ding down the avenue in a southerly direction in order to escape detection & possible repercussions?

Come to think of it, I should be writing 'formal styles and informal styles', in this entry – because there's more to formality than the simple difference between a very formal style and a very informal one. It's like clothing, in a way. You have clothes that are very formal (such as a suit) or very informal (such as jeans with holes in the knees), but the ones you use most often are probably somewhere in between (such as a casual top). Similarly, you can have several different levels of formality in language. It's interesting to take some examples of spoken or written language, and try to put them onto a scale running from 'most formal' to 'least formal'. Where would you put the style of this book, for instance? Near the informal end? Correct. But how do you know that?

 colloquial speech; style; usage; variety

formula (**fawm**-yuh-luh), plural formulae (**fawm**-yuh-lee)

God save the Queen! Long live Bloggs!
Good morning. The more, the merrier.
Your very good health. Many happy returns.

Can you see what's interesting about these sentences? Some of them look quite normal. *God save the Queen*, for instance, seems to have the same pattern as *The goalie saves a penalty*. In fact, it isn't at all the same. Notice, for a start, that the sentence isn't 'God *saves* the Queen'; it seems to be short for 'May God save the Queen'. You can't shorten the *goalie* sentence like that. **The goalie save a penalty*. Not possible. Or look at it from a different point of view. You can change the *goalie* sentence round: *The goalie has saved a penalty, The goalie likes saving penalties*. You can't do this to our other sentence. *God has saved the Queen? God likes saving Queens?* In fact, you can't do anything to *God save the Queen*. It's a sentence with a fixed structure. You can't change the order of the words, add extra words or endings, or leave words or endings out. In short, it's a linguistic **formula**. Sentences of this kind are sometimes called **formulaic speech** (pronounced fawm-yuh-**lay**-ik). Try changing the others, and see how far you get. *Many returns?* No. *Bad morning?* No. *Your good health?* Ah, that allows a little change. *Short live Bloggs?* No. Carry on.

 block language    major sentence

full stop

It's only a tiny punctuation mark, but it has an awful lot of names. Apart from **full stop**, it's known as a **period**, a **full point** – and even a **dot**! Its main job is well known: it is used to show that a sentence has come to an end. Notice how in print there's always a bit of extra space following this use of the full stop. That's important, as it helps to distinguish the sentence use of the full stop from a different use, to mark an abbreviation, as in *B.C.* Notice that the space after an abbreviation full stop isn't as large as that following a sentence full stop. Look around and see if you can see any other uses of the full stop. Here's one: it can be used in writing the time or the date. *8.25, 6.9.1990*. And I wonder if you can think of the one case in English when you're allowed to have a string of three full stops, one after the other . . .

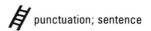 punctuation; sentence

function word see **grammatical word**

64

future tense

Josephine is leaving tomorrow.
Josephine is going to leave.
Josephine is about to leave.
Josephine will leave.
Josephine shall leave in the morning.
Josephine is to leave tonight.

English gives us a surprisingly large number of ways to talk about the future. You've just read some of them. But the one thing it doesn't do is give us a special ending to add to the verb in order to express future meaning. This does happen in French, for example, where there's a separate **future tense** ending. English doesn't have a future tense like this. The nearest we get in English to a simple future meaning is with the words *will* and

shall, and some grammarians actually call these the 'future tense' forms of English. But beware! The words *will* and *shall* have other meanings too. They don't always express future time. Look at the way *will* is used in this sentence, for instance, and ask 'What does it mean?'

Oil will float on water.

Does it mean that oil is going to float on water only *in the future*? No. It means that oil *always* floats on water. It will in the future, it does now, and it has in the past. So, be careful with *will* and *shall*. They're not always a way of getting back to the

 tense   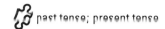 past tense; present tense

gender

This entry is all about sex. Well, nearly. But I shall be very polite. (Who said 'Shame'?) And in fact I intend to begin with a very tasteful example:

My uncle is a monk. He and his brothers are men I admire.
My aunt is a nun. She and her sisters are women I admire.

What's happening here? Try mixing up the sentences, and you'll find out:

*My uncle is a nun. He and his brother are women I admire.

That sounds a bit more interesting, but unfortunately all I want to talk about just now is the grammar of these sentences. Words like *monk*, *sister*, *he*, and *she* tell you about the sex of the people we're talking about. Only a few nouns do this in English. If the sentence had been:

That person is a doctor/writer/friend/foreigner . . .

you wouldn't know whether it was a man or a woman, would you? Whenever we get words that give us information about the sex of what's being referred to, we talk about **gender**. Some other gender words are *himself*, *bachelor*, *Mister*, *king*, *empress*, and *bride*. Male words are usually called **masculine gender**; female words are usually called **feminine gender**; and those which are neither male nor female are called **neuter gender** (pronounced **nyoo**-tuh) or **impersonal gender**. This last group includes such words as *stone*, *table*, *cup*, and *hydrogen sulphide*. You can tell the gender of these words, too, if you know what to look out for:

Here's the cup which I bought yesterday. It was expensive.

Do you see the *which* and the *it*? They show that you're using an impersonal word – one which is neither masculine nor feminine. You wouldn't have:

*Here's the cup who I bought yesterday. He was expensive.

All fairly obvious? So far. Things start to get interesting when you realise that some people can actually be called *it* and some objects can be called *he* or *she*! Have you ever heard sentences like these:

It's a boy!
She steers beautifully at 70.
England is proud of her policemen.

And what do we do with animals? We tend to call our pets *he* and *she*, but spiders and ants tend to be *it*, for most people. And our dog is *he* when he's good and *it* when he's bad!

GOVERNMENT WORD WARNING! If you've studied French or German, or certain other languages, you'll have come across gender before. In those languages, *all* nouns have gender – masculine and feminine in French, and neuter as well in German. But there's a big difference between those languages and English. In French and German the gender of the noun doesn't necessarily tell you

M'sieur – the cow
he is coming!

anything about sex. A table, for instance, is masculine in German (*der Tisch*) and feminine in French (*la table*). You have to learn the gender of each noun when you learn the noun. It's one of the big problems, isn't it? English nouns don't work like that. (Did I hear someone say 'Thank goodness'?) For the most part, their gender follows what happens in nature (it's a language with **natural gender**), whereas French and German nouns follow the rules of grammar (they're languages with **grammatical gender**).

 noun   personification   animate

genitive case see **case**

genre (**zhawn**-ruh)

ALI: Do you write poetry?
DEB: No, I write plays.
ALI: Comedies?
DEB: No, tragedies. What about you?
ALI: Oh, I write short stories. Horrors, mainly.
DEB: Hmm!

Think about some of the other things you can write – essays, romantic novels, prayers, science fiction stories . . . All of these are well-known types of writing. Each type involves a particular approach, content, or style. You expect poetry to be written in shortish lines. You expect romantic novels to have a happy ending. You expect detective novels to have a murder at the beginning, and at least a couple more before the end. These distinct varieties of literature are called **genres**. This is a French word meaning 'kind' or 'type', and it's usually pronounced in a French way. Dictionaries and encyclopedias are examples of other genres. This book is an example of a genre, too – but not one that's easy to define, as it's a mixture of dictionary and encyclopedia.

style; variety   haiku; text

grammar (**gra**-muh)
grammarian (gruh-**mair**-ee-uhn)
grammatical (gruh-**ma**-ti-kuhl)

Sort these sentences out into two piles:

A   The cat sat on the dog.
B   Town to going are boys the.
C   Of a car two see wheels I can.
D   I can see a little tree.
E   Jimmy likes eating chips.
F   Everyone Sam dog knows a called.

Did you get A, D, E and B, C, F? If you did, how were you able to reach that conclusion? I didn't tell you how. But then, I didn't need to. You already know which are possible sentences in English and which aren't. You speak the language. You learned the rules, without realising it, when you were little. When you study **grammar**, all you're trying to do is bring to the front of your mind everything about the structure of the language that you take for granted. You're trying to write down, in a clear way, everything that is in your head about the way sentences are made and how they hang together in a sequence. The people who write grammars are called **grammarians**. Grammarians work out the rules you have to follow in order to make sentences that everyone will happily use and understand. If a sentence follows the rules of the language, you call it **grammatical**. If it doesn't, you call it **ungrammatical**. *The TV set is broken* is a grammatical sentence, although an unfortunate fact. *Repaired set is TV the* sounds more promising, but it's definitely ungrammatical. The asterisk is a way of showing that a sentence is ungrammatical.

Actually, I cheated a bit when I gave you the list of sentences just now. I didn't put any problem cases in. In fact there are several types of sentence in English which aren't clearly grammatical *or* clearly ungrammatical. They're somewhere in between. Some people would put them into the grammatical pile; some would put them into the ungrammatical pile; and some wouldn't be able to make up their mind. Here's one example:

She asked me to definitely answer by Friday.

Some people think this isn't correct English. Rather, they say, it should be:

She asked me to answer definitely by Friday.

Why? Because (they say) you shouldn't put a word like *definitely* (an adverb) between the *to* and the verb (the infinitive). To do so is to 'split the infinitive', and this they think is wrong.

The split infinitive construction is just one of many types of sentence which cause problems of usage. And when people start arguing about such sentences, the arguments can go on for ages, and get very emotional. You may have seen letters in the newspapers, or heard letters read out on the radio, complaining about what the writer calls 'bad grammar'. But other people can't see what the fuss is all about. Why are opinions so divided? It's partly because of the changing way people have been taught about English in school. Once upon a time, students would be severely criticised, or even physically punished, if they used a split infinitive. It was held to be a mark of good education to avoid them. More recently, this kind of grammar hasn't been taught in schools, so younger people don't know about the issue. In the 1990s, grammar is back in schools but with a big difference. These days, teachers aren't so likely to tell you that you must/mustn't use these problem constructions. They're much more likely to discuss with you *why* people have different feelings about them, and point out to you *when* it would be appropriate or inappropriate to use the different versions.

Questions of usage are extremely interesting, because they are questions about the way society sees itself. I hope you enjoy discussing them. But be prepared for some strong opinions, one way or the other, if you ask older adults what they think about it all! You'll find that many people aren't very tolerant, and there are some intriguing views around. Once, on a radio programme, I got a letter which said, 'Children who split infinitives are much more likely to go around breaking shop windows'. What do you think about that?

 appropriate; clause; inflection; parts of speech; phrase; sentence; syntax; usage; word

grammatical word and lexical word (**lek**-si-kuhl)

Sort these ten words out into two piles of five:

table   the   man   eat   of   and   am   elephant   suitcase   is

If you put *the, of, and, am,* and *is* into one pile, and the remaining words into the other, then you saw what I was after. (If you didn't, it doesn't matter. Just read on.) What's the difference between these two groups? Try telling someone what each word means, and you'll see. *Table*? No problem. *Eat*? No problem. *The*? Problem! *Of*? Problem! There are several dozen words in English which don't seem to have any clear meaning at all. Their job seems to be to link together the words which *do* seem to have meaning. In short, they show you the grammar of the sentence – like this:

The – was – in the –.

Without them, the meaningful words don't make much sense:

car damaged street.

But put them together, and bingo!

The car was damaged in the street.

Because the job of these 'little' words is to show the structure, or grammar, of the sentence, they're usually called **grammatical words**. You'll also hear them called **function words**, because they show you how the other words function in the sentence. These other words – the ones with a clearer meaning – are often called **lexical words**, because they're part of the real vocabulary, or 'lexicon', of the language. They're also called **content words**, because they're full of 'content', or meaning. Now, go through this entry and see if you can tell which are the grammatical words and which are the lexical words.

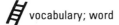 vocabulary; word    grammar; sentence

hyphen (**hie**-fuhn)

You know the problem. You're writing an essay, and you get to the end of a line, and the word you want to write won't fit the space you've got left. So what can you do? You have three choices. You can try to cram it in (I wouldn't advise this – it looks awful). You can leave a space, and write the word at the beginning of the next line. Or you can put half the word in, and finish it off on the next line. If you choose this last solution, then you need to show what you've done by using the punctuation mark called the **hyphen**. A hyphen shows you that a word has been divided into two parts. You'll find it quite often at the end of a line, especially when you're reading a book that has its right-hand margin straight. (This book isn't like that. My right-hand margins dip in and out, don't they? You won't find any hyphens there. Why? It makes a book easier to read, if you don't keep chopping words in half.) And you'll also find hyphens in the middle of certain words. Two-part numbers, for instance, have a hyphen in the middle, when they're written out as words: *thirty-three*, *two-fifths*. And here are some other examples:

mother-in-law   do-it-yourself   ex-footballer
green-eyed   U-turn   runner-up

Are you up-to-date and on-the-ball about this?

⌗ punctuation   ⌘ affix; compound word

Oh lor, it's the Kennington-Gores

idiom (**id**-ee-uhm)

What do you notice about these sentences?

Matthew drinks like a fish.
Jock's got a flea in his ear.
Agnes wiped the floor with Peter.
Judy is the fly in the ointment.

No marks for noticing that they've all got words beginning with *f*. It's something else. Take one of the sentences, and try to work out what it says by looking at the meanings of the separate words. You won't succeed. If we look in Jock's ear, will we really find a flea? Is Judy really pretending to be a fly in an enormous jar of ointment? Is poor old Peter really being used as a mop? Not a bit. In each case, the sentence means something different from what the individual words seem to be saying. When this happens, we say that the sentence contains an **idiom**. There are thousands and thousands of idioms in English. Some are quite simple, containing just two words: *drink up* doesn't mean 'drink in an upwards direction' – it means 'finish off drinking'. Some are quite complicated: *two can play at that game*. And, of course, you can have several idioms in a single sentence. I hope you won't fly off the handle if I screw up my courage and put all my cards on the table. Are you looking daggers at me?

⌘ figure of speech; literal

illiterate see literate

imagery (**im**-uh-juh-ree)

The autumn trees were a curtain of gold.
The waves crashed angrily against the breakwater.
The clouds rested on the mountain like a silk tablecloth.

I woke up feeling poetic today – which is just as well, as I have to
write this entry. An 'image' is a likeness or picture of something.
You can see what the images are in these sentences – the curtain of
gold, crashing angrily, the silk tablecloth resting. If you don't like
those images, you can make up your own. How else might clouds
rest on a mountain, for instance? Like an old man in an overcoat?
Like Dracula approaching a victim? There's no limit to the number
of images you can think up. And when you use vivid, pictorial
language to express your meaning, it's known as **imagery**. Usually,
you find the most dramatic and memorable imagery in poetry, and
in plays and stories too. But everyday conversation also makes use
of imagery. *Fred left the shop, running like a bat out of hell. She looked like
a ghost. He was as white as a sheet*. In fact, it's almost impossible to
speak and write without imagery of some kind. I hope that's clear as
crystal.

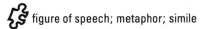 figure of speech; metaphor; simile

indefinite article see article

indentation or indention

Take a look at a page from some books you've been reading recently
(not this one). Have you noticed how, every so often, one of the
lines starts a little way in from the left-hand edge of the page? This is
called **indentation** or **indention**. It's mainly used to mark the
beginning of a new paragraph, but you'll sometimes see it in other
places too, such as when the author wants a line of print to stand
out in some way – like this:

This is an example of indentation being used in front of an example.

(Have you noticed that the designer of this book hasn't used that style, for showing examples? How has he made my examples stand out?) In dictionaries and encyclopedias, you'll often find that the page has been designed 'back to front'. The headwords, at the beginning of each entry, start at the left-hand margin, and everything else is indented. This is called **reverse indentation**. I'll give you two seconds to find a page in a book which uses reverse indentation. Got it?

 paragraph

indirect object see **direct object**

indirect speech see **direct speech**

infinitive (in-**fin**-uh-tiv)

What have William Shakespeare and Arthur Bloomingpant got in common? They each wrote one of the following sentences (no marks for guessing who wrote which):

To be or not to be, that is the question.
I dunno whether to go to the pictures or to get a video out.

The answer is that both sentences have verbs in their **infinitive** form: *to be* (twice), *to go*, and *to get*. What's the infinitive form? It's the basic form of the verb – the simplest form – the form without any endings. Compare these: *walk, walks, walking, walked*. Which is the basic form? *Walk*, of course. That's the infinitive. How can you check? You can put the word *to* in front of it. *To walk*. That's another way of showing that you've got an infinitive. When infinitives are used with the word *to* in front of them, they're called (believe it or not) ***to*-infinitives**. When they are used without the *to*, they're called **bare infinitives**. In some sentences, you can have both. In Arthur's sentence, above, you can leave out the *to* in front of *get*, and the sentence still sounds acceptable:

I dunno whether to go to the pictures or get a video out.

(But you can't leave out the first *to*! Try it and see.)

 verb

inflection (in-**flek**-shuhn)

I like a quick frog.   I liked quick frogs.   He likes quicker frogs.

What am I doing (apart from going mad)? I'm playing about with word endings. (Well, it passes the time of day.) These endings tell you something about the way the words are being used in the sentence. Add an *s* to *frog*, and you change from one ('singular') to more than one ('plural'). Add an *s* to *like* and you change from 'me' liking (the 'first person') to 'he' or 'she' liking (the 'third person'). Add a *d* to *like* and you change from now ('present tense') to then ('past tense'). Add an *er* to *quick*, and you change from ordinary quickness (the 'absolute' form) to greater quickness (the 'comparative' form). Endings of this kind are called **inflections**. There are very few inflections in English (compared with such languages as French, German, or Welsh). If you look through this entry, you'll find another one in *playing* and *being*.

 affix; word   comparative; noun; verb   morphology

interjection (in-ter-**jek**-shuhn)

Coo! Ugh! Aaargh! Tut tut. Phew! Oops! Aha! Eh? Shhh. Psst! Boo!

What have all these words got in common? Well, are they words at all? *Shhh* and *Aaargh* don't seem to be the sort of thing you could look up in a dictionary. They're more like noises than words. And some of the noises aren't even sounds that are part of normal English pronunciation. The sound of *Ugh* is usually made somewhere at the back of the throat. *Tut tut* is a pair of click noises. So why do we make all these noises? They're used to express our emotions, such as surprise, pain, and disgust. They stand on their own, and don't form part of a sentence. We don't say things like *I've just oopsed* or *My ugh is horrible*. Words of this kind are called **interjections**.

 parts of speech

74

intransitive verb see **transitive verb**

inverted commas

'No, no!', Hilary cried, in a tearful voice. 'I'll tell the vicar!'

There are two voices here. Hilary's and mine (I'm the one telling the story). How do you know which is which? The punctuation tells you. The marks which surround the bits Hilary said are called **inverted commas**, because the opening mark looks like an upside-down comma. It's usually printed like this: ' – but in this book the designer has used a simplified shape: '. They're also called **speech marks** or **quotation marks** (**quotes**, for short), because they enclose a piece taken from real speech – in other words, a quotation. Sometimes just one mark is used at the beginning and end of the quoted speech – **single** inverted commas. Sometimes you get pairs of marks – **double** inverted commas. Here's the same sentence using double inverted commas:

"No, no!", Hilary cried, in a tearful voice. "I'll tell the vicar!"

Both styles are widely used, but British books generally prefer to use single inverted commas. You can also have both styles in the same sentence, if you want to put one quotation inside another quotation – like this:

Mike said, 'I heard Wain call out "She's here" in a surprised tone'.
Mike said, "I heard Wain call out 'She's here' in a surprised tone".

In the first case, you've got double quotes inside single quotes. In the second case, it's the other way round. It doesn't matter which way you do it, as long as you keep the two voices apart.

There are some other uses of inverted commas which you need to know about. For instance, inverted commas can be used to single out a word that's being used in a technical way: look at the entry on **inflection**, and you'll see several examples of this. Also, I use inverted commas a lot in this book when I'm telling you what something means: look at the entry on **idiom** and you'll find a good example of this. Some people use them to show titles: this book is called 'Language A–Z'. And lastly, inverted commas can show you that a word has a special meaning – especially when you're being humorous or sarcastic about something. They're sometimes called 'scare quotes', in this use, because they're telling you to be careful – watch out for the special meaning here. Can you feel the difference between these two sentences?

Rupert came in wearing his new trousers.
Rupert came in wearing his new 'trousers'.

Whatever he's wearing, in the second sentence, they certainly aren't ordinary trousers!

 punctuation

irrelevance see **relevance**

jargon (**jah**-guhn)

CUSTOMER: What's wrong with my robot?
SALESMAN: I'm afraid the link sprocket in the anterior upper arm assembly is no longer interconnecting horizontally with the rotating posterior mechanism.
CUSTOMER: Eh?
SALESMAN: His arm's broken.

I expect you had a problem too. The salesman knows what he's talking about – but the rest of us don't, because we don't understand all his technical words, or **jargon**. Every specialised subject has got its own jargon. Chemistry, maths, geography . . . This book is all about the jargon of English language study. Each sport has its jargon, too. If you don't know anything about cricket, for instance, words like *googly* and *third man* will be just as unintelligible as *link sprocket* and *posterior mechanism*. When a group of specialists are talking together, they use jargon quite naturally, because it helps them to be precise. What's bad is when they use jargon to people who *don't* know what it means. Can you think of people who might use jargon in this way? Doctors sometimes do. And garage mechanics. And lawyers. Any others?

 vocabulary    style; usage

language

This book is all about **language** – the English language. But we mustn't be so busy finding out about English that we forget to ask what a language is in the first place. First and foremost, it's a way of communicating with each other. But what a way! It can express far more meanings than any other way of communicating – such as by using gestures or facial expressions. There seems to be no limit to what we can say, using language. Hundreds of new words come into English every year. People keep making up new sentences that no one has ever used before. It's often been said that children never master anything more complex than their first language. You'll quickly get a sense of just how vast the whole business is if you reflect on the following four points:

- Language has a very complex structure – all the sounds of speech, all the spellings, all the ways of building up words, all the sentence patterns, all the vocabulary. (That's why you need books like this one – to help sort out what goes on within this structure.)
- There isn't just one side to learning your language, but four – you have to learn to understand it, to speak it, and eventually to read it and write it. If you're deaf, you can also learn to sign it, using sign language.
- Language has a very wide range of uses – to communicate ideas, persuade, command, question, hurt, argue, pray . . . Can you carry on this list?
- Language varies enormously from one time and place to another – all the dialects and accents, all the styles of speech and writing.

When you think of all this, it's truly remarkable how quickly children come to learn their language. Next time you listen to a five-year-old speaking English, remember to be impressed!

 accent; bilingual; communication; dialect; first language; grammar; sentence; usage; vocabulary

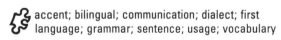 lingua franca; metalanguage

lexical word see **grammatical word**

lexicon see **vocabulary**

limerick (**lim**-uh-rik)

There was a Swiss farmer called Cass
Whose donkey fell down a crevasse

Can you finish this off? If you can, you know about limericks. A **limerick** is a verse which has five lines. The first, second, and fifth lines rhyme, and each has three rhythmical beats. The third and fourth lines also rhyme, but they only have two rhythmical beats each. The rhythm is very bouncy: te-**tum**-te-te-**tum**-te-te-**tum**. The first lines often start in the same way: 'There was a young man from Dundee', 'There was a young lady from Paris'. No one knows how limericks began. They became very popular 100 years ago. Presumably it has something to do with the town of Limerick in Ireland. Maybe an old Irish song started the idea. But wherever they started, there are now thousands of them. Oh, and I should add that limericks are often a bit rude – but you probably knew that already. Now, where was I?

So he went to the zoo
And asked 'What shall I do?'
They said: 'Yodel: I can't find my ass'.

rhyme; rhythm

78

literal (**lit**-uh-ruhl)

DAN: I had thousands of chips for lunch.
FRAN: Don't be silly. I'm sure you had only about 100, at the most.

Fran, of course, was right. If you actually counted the number of chips in Dan's paper bag, I doubt whether there'd be more than 100. (I've never counted, actually. Have you?) But Dan was too hungry to count. All he could see was a lot of chips. So he said 'thousands'. He might have said 'millions'. It wouldn't matter. All he's doing is saying 'a lot' as dramatically as he can. But Fran isn't having any of this. She's decided to be awkward (well, they had a row last week), so she takes Dan's words in their true dictionary meaning. If you take language to mean exactly what it says, then you're taking it **literally**. Here are some other exaggerations which we don't usually take literally. You're tired, after a cross-country run, so when someone asks you to take a message to Mr Smith's class, which is in the next building, you say *But it's miles to Block B!* And I'm sure you've heard parents say things like *It's months since you last cut your toenails*. Idioms, too, aren't taken literally. *It's raining cats and dogs.* (Call the kennels?) *It's bucketing down.* (Put your helmets on?)

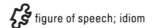 figure of speech; idiom   hyperbole

literate (**li**-tuh-ruht) and illiterate (i-**li**-tuh-ruht)

You can read. (If not, put this book down right now!) You can also, I hope, write. If you *can* read and write, then you're **literate**. If you can't, you're **illiterate**. Actually, there are a very large number of people in the world who can't read and write – especially in some of the countries of Africa and Asia. And even in this country, there are several million adults who have great difficulty reading and writing. Many can read and write a little, but can't cope with anything complicated. Fighting illiteracy is a big problem, and you may have seen that in Britain there's a national literacy campaign to try to help people in need. You yourself might like to help, one day. Ask your teacher, or your local librarian, if you want to find out more.

 alphabet; punctuation

loan word see **borrowing**

logogram (**log**-oh-gram)

4 + 4 = 8

No, this isn't a maths lesson. It's still English. Symbols like 4, 8, +, and = are interesting, because they stand for whole words: 'plus' or 'and', 'equals' or 'is', 'four', and 'eight'. A symbol which stands for a whole word is called a **logogram**. Apart from the numbers, and various scientific symbols, there aren't many logograms in English. The commonest ones are the sign for 'and' (&), the sign for 'at' (@), and the signs for money values (£, $). You'll see them on a computer keyboard. Notice how these signs can cross the boundary between languages. 4 + 4 = 8 is the same in French, German, Hungarian, Swedish . . . I bet you didn't know you knew so many languages!

 alphabet

lower-case letter see **upper case**

masculine see **gender**

metaphor (**me**-tuh-faw)

SHARON: The ship ploughed through the rough waves.
ME: Eh? Not possible. Ploughs go in fields.

SHARON: The flames from the bonfire danced high in the air.
ME: Sorry. Not possible. People dance, not flames.

SHARON: I've just cooked up this great idea.
ME: Out of the question. You cook food, not ideas.

I think that, by now, you've gathered that I'm having Sharon on. Anyone who really did think like this would be missing the point. So what *is* the point? Well, take the first sentence. To think of a ship as 'ploughing' through the sea brings quite a vivid and powerful picture to mind. You think of a plough, and what it does – how it goes strongly and steadily in a straight line. Then you think of the ship in the sea, and in your mind you transfer some of the images of

the plough to the ship. What you're doing is describing one idea using the language belonging to a different idea, so that you come to see a likeness between them. Plough-language for ships. Dance-language for flames. Cooking-language for ideas. We call these likenesses of thought **metaphors**. Great poets have thought up some marvellous metaphors. Here's Shakespeare, writing about the dead Julius Caesar.

Thou art the ruins of the noblest man.

What's the thought-likeness here? Ruins. The sad remains of a great building – now applied to a person. But don't think that only great writers are allowed to use metaphors. Ordinary people use thousands of metaphors every day. We often insult each other with metaphors (*You cow!, You dirty pig!*). Do you know someone who's fighting a disease? Or sitting on her money? Or building up his confidence? You'll hear dozens before you hit the hay tonight – if you keep your ears open for them.

figure of speech   imagery; personification; simile   metonymy

We're having a whip-round for the vicar's retirement present

metre (**mee**-tuh)
metrical (**me**-tri-kuhl)

Beat a drum out loud, beat a drum out
        loud
You can listen to the beating of the drum
        out loud

If you say these lines of poetry aloud, in a nice jerky way, they will actually remind you of the way a drum sounds when someone is beating it. The words have been carefully chosen so that when they go together they make up a drum-like rhythm. The rhythmical pattern you hear in lines of poetry is called the **metre** (don't mix this spelling up with **meter**, which you'll find in *parking meter* and other measuring instruments). You can tap out the metrical patterns with your fingers, or write them down using different symbols for the heavy beats and the light beats. Here are the above two lines written out in a '**tum**-te-**tum**' way:

te-te-**tum-tum-tum**, te-te-**tum-tum-tum**

te-te-**tum**-te-te-te-**tum**-te-te-te-**tum**-tum-
        tum

Some lines of poetry have a very obvious and regular metre. Here are a few lines, taken from different poems, to show you some of the possibilities:

This is the night train, crossing the
        border . . .
The folk that live in Liverpool, their heart
        is in their boots . . .
The curfew tolls the knell of parting
        day . . .
What of soul was left, I wonder, when the
        kissing had to stop?

And here is a line of poetry where the metre isn't so regular:

I have measured out my life with coffee
        spoons . . .

 rhythm    prosody; stress

monolingual see **bilingual**

monologue see **dialogue**

motherese

Who said this?

Oh dear, what a mess! What a mess! That doggie has made a big mess, hasn't he! Naughty doggie! You give him big spanks. Big spanks. There. Will he be good doggie now?

I don't mean who exactly, of course! I mean what sort of person? A mother, talking to her little child? Correct. It's a very curious style,

isn't it? Very simple sentences, sometimes with words left out. Special endings added on to some of the words. Some of the phrases repeated several times. And there's something else – though you can't see it from the way I've written it down: the distinctive melody of the speech – almost like singing, at times. Of course, not all mothers talk like this, but a very large number do. The style is called **motherese** (that's *mother* + *-ese*, as in Chin*ese*, Japan*ese* . . .), but actually, this term is a bit misleading, because you'll hear fathers say similar things – and grannies, and nannies, and most of us, in fact. Anyone taking care of a young child is likely to lapse into this way of talking – so it's often called **caretaker speech**.

 baby talk

mother tongue see **first language**

multilingual see **bilingual**

negative (**neg**-uh-tiv)
negation (nuh-**gay**-shuhn)

No. Nope. Never. Not at all. No way. Won't. Can't.

And I only wanted to borrow a pound. Stingy blighter. But I got a good range of 'no' words, didn't I? A word or ending which expresses the meaning 'no' is called a **negative**. A sentence with a negative word is a negative sentence. Its opposites are **positive** or **affirmative**, which are used for sentences that have a 'yes' meaning. The commonest way of expressing negative meaning (or **negation**) in English is to use the word *not* or the ending *n't*, along with a verb. Here are a few negative sentences, and their positive opposites:

I am not ready.	I am ready.
You must not sleep in.	You must sleep in.
I don't want anything to eat.	I want something to eat.

Did you notice what happened in that last pair of sentences? As soon as the *not* disappeared, the word *anything* changed to *something*. We don't say **I want anything to eat*. We generally use *anything* only in negative sentences, and *something* in positive ones.

NEVER NOT NO SMOKING NOHOW

GOVERNMENT WORD WARNING! Most dialects of English allow sentences with two negative markers in them, like this:

I have**n't** done **nothing**.
She has**n't** got **no** change.

This is called a **double negative** construction. Sometimes you'll even hear three or more negatives in the same sentence:

Jim won't never get no money from me nohow.

You can see what's happening. The more negative words you add on, the more forceful the 'no' meaning becomes. BUT – and this is the biggest 'but' in this book – the double negative is widely criticised if you use it in standard English, especially in writing. Standard English speakers prefer:

I haven't done **anything**.
She hasn't got **any** change.

So, be careful.

 affirmative; verb

neologism (nee-**ol**-uh-jiz-uhm)

Our new perfume is really girl-friendly.
That's a mega-trendy coat.
There's a swimathon at the local pool on Sunday
This is your soundsational radio station!
Stop that Rambo-like behaviour!

I've heard every one of those words in the last few weeks, but I don't think you'll find *girl-friendly*, *mega-trendy*, and the others in the dictionary just yet. They're new words, recently invented. New words or phrases in a language are called **neologisms**, or **coinages**. Hundreds of them come into the language every year. Not all of them stay for long, though. Some become very fashionable, then they die away. People stop using them. Others stay for years, and may become a permanent part of the language. It's impossible to predict which words will live and which will die. Will *Yuppy* still be with us in ten years' time? Place your bets.

vocabulary   affix

neuter see **gender**

non-standard English see **standard English**

nonverbal communication see **communication**

noun

A **noun** is a word whose job is naming, or labelling. So what does a noun name? People, places, objects, concepts, ideas . . . anything you want to talk about, really. You'll realise, therefore, that there are a lot of nouns about. And that's where the grammarian's problem starts. The nouns don't all work in sentences in the same way. They fall into different groups, depending on the way they're used.

- The most important division is into **proper nouns** and **common nouns**. Proper nouns are written with a capital letter at the beginning, such as in *Dora*, *Derby*, and *December*. All the others are common nouns, such as *horse*, *happiness*, and *hydrogen*. Look at the entry on **proper noun** for more information about them.
- The common nouns are of two main types. Most of them are **count nouns**, such as *car* and *horse* – you can 'count' them, and say *two cars*, *three horses*, and so on. The others are **non-count nouns**, such as *warmth* and *mud* – you can't count them, or say **two warmths* and **three muds*.
- You can divide all the common nouns from another point of view: there are **concrete nouns** and **abstract nouns**.

Concrete nouns are nouns which refer to things that you can see, feel, measure, and so on – nouns such as *cat*, *carrot*, *computer*, and *carbon-dioxide*. Abstract nouns are nouns which refer to notions that you can't observe or measure, such as *music*, *mercy*, *muddle*, and *mood*.

So, when you're analysing nouns, there are three chief questions to ask about each one. First, decide whether it's proper or common. If it's proper, there's nothing more to do. But if it's common, then you can ask two more questions. Is it count or non-count? Is it concrete or abstract? Here are a few to start you off:

Fred	proper
egg	count, concrete
noun	count, abstract
wealth	non-count, abstract
mud	non-count, concrete

Try going through the nouns in this entry, and see what comes up.

parts of speech   proper noun

²abstract noun; animate; collective noun; count noun; determiner; irregular

noun phrase

Games are fun.
Computer games are fun.
New computer games are fun.
New cheap computer games are fun.
New cheap computer games from America are fun.
The new cheap computer games which have come from America are fun.
Some of the new cheap computer games which have come from North America are fun.

You can carry on making this sentence longer, if you want to. All you have to do is say something more about *games*. *Games* is definitely the chief word in the phrase. It's what the phrase is all about. *Games* is a noun – so what sort of phrase is it? Exactly. A **noun phrase**. Here are some of the noun phrases I've already used in this entry (I've made the chief word stand out):

this **sentence** the chief **word** the **phrase** a **noun**
some of the noun **phrases** this **entry**

Most noun phrases are quite short, in everyday speech – often consisting of just an article (*the* or *a*) and a noun. But if you look in textbooks, it can be a different story. Try finding the chief word in this horrendous noun phrase:

Not quite all of the green mixture which was left at the bottom of the test tube has evaporated.

What's evaporating? The mixture.

noun; phrase

number

You probably think you know all about this term already, and I wouldn't blame you. Numbers? Easy: one, two, three, four . . . Your maths teacher will have told you all about them. But in grammar, the term *number* is used in a rather different way. It's mainly used for talking about how nouns work in the language. There's **singular** number, where the noun means 'one'; and there's **plural** number, where the noun means 'more than one'. *The computer* means a single computer. *The computers* means several computers. The usual way of showing that a noun means 'more than one' is to add a special ending – the plural ending. For most nouns in written English, this is an *s* – *computers, cats, cows, cottages*. (In speech, notice how the *-s* ending is pronounced in three different ways. In *cats* it sounds like the *s* in *soup*. In *cows* it sounds like the *z* in *zoo*. And in *cottages* the ending sounds like the word *is*.) There is also quite a large number of nouns where the plural is made differently. These are the **irregular nouns**. Here's a selection of irregular plurals (I'll put the singular form in brackets):

calves (calf)   feet (foot)   children (child)   larvae (larva)
knives (knife)   men (man)   mice (mouse)   oases (oasis)

There are even some nouns which don't have any ending at all, in the plural: the singular and the plural are the same. *One sheep – lots of sheep. One cod – lots of cod.*

GOVERNMENT WORD WARNING! There are some nouns which look as if they're plural, because they've got an *-s* ending, but the language is playing a trick on you, because they're really singular. *News* is an example. We say *The news is on at 10 o'clock*, not **The news are on at 10 o'clock. Darts* is another. *Darts is a popular game*, not **Darts are a popular game.*

ANOTHER WORD WARNING! There are also some nouns which look as though they're singular, because they don't have an *-s* ending, but the language is playing another trick on you, because they're really plural. *Police* is one example. We say *The police are outside*, not **The police is outside. Cattle* is another. *The cattle were in the field*, not **The cattle was in the field.*

 noun   concord    collective noun; count noun

object (**ob**-jekt)

Rajiv posted a letter.
Marian smashed a cup.
The cat scratched the furniture.
The dog ate a bone.

What actions have taken place in these sentences? Posting, smashing, scratching, and eating. Now, which persons or things have been most closely affected by these actions? What gets posted? Rajiv or the letter? The letter, of course. And what gets smashed? Marian or the cup? The cup. In a sentence, the thing most affected by the action of the verb is called the **object**. In the other two sentences, *the furniture* and *a bone* are the objects of the verbs. Objects usually follow their verbs. Just occasionally, you can have an object coming at the beginning of a sentence. Imagine someone saying, 'But Marian smashed a plate, didn't she?' 'No,' you reply. 'A *cup* Marian smashed!' But don't expect there to be an object in every sentence. There are lots of sentences which don't need one. *This entry is finishing. I'm going.*

📏 clause   🧩 direct object; transitive verb

objective case see **case**

overextension (oh-vuhr-eks-**ten**-shuhn)

There ball, says little Peter, aged two, pointing to his football. Splendid. No problems here. But then you hear him say *There ball*, pointing to a plate. And at bedtime, he looks at the sky and says *Ball!*, pointing to the moon! What's going on? You can work it out if you think what a ball, a plate, and a moon have in common. They're all round. Peter thinks the word *ball* means 'something round', so he uses it for anything he sees of that shape. When young children do this – and they all do – it's called **overextension**, because part of a meaning has been taken too far (it's been 'over-extended'). Sometimes it's the shape of an object that causes the overextension, as in the moon example. Sometimes it's the sound an object makes, or its colour, or how it feels. I know a little girl, Sarah, aged two and a quarter, who calls all animals *woof* – whether they're dogs or not. (I don't know what her cat thinks of that situation. I can imagine what Garfield would say.) Overextensions don't last for ever. By the age of two and a half, or so, most children have learned to

tell the difference between the different types of round object, animal, and so on. But while they're overextending word meanings, they're at an important stage of normal development – and it's a fascinating one to study.

🧩 underextension

palindrome (**pa**-lin-drohm)

Spell *Eve*. Now spell it backwards. Notice anything? They're the same. Now spell *madam* in both directions. Same both ways again. Words and phrases which read the same in both directions are called **palindromes** – a Greek word which means 'running back again'. In fact, you can go beyond words and phrases, and have whole sentences which are palindromes – but, of course, the longer the sentence, the more difficult it is to make the palindrome work. Here are a few shortish ones, and a longish one:

Madam, I'm Adam.
Adam, I'm Ada.
Draw, o coward!
Nurse, I spy gypsies. Run!
Doc, note, I dissent. A fast never prevents
   a fatness. I diet on cod.

Why not launch a competition to see who can make the longest palindrome? You can give a copy of this book as the first prize. And two copies as the second prize.

 word games

pangram (**pan**-gram)

Here's a nice little task, to while away a wet evening. Write a sentence 26 letters long, with each letter of the alphabet being used only once. You can have as many words as you like, but each word must be a proper English word, and the sentence must make sense. If you can do this, you've made a perfect **pangram**. It sounds easy, but in fact it's very difficult. Here's one person's attempt:

The five boxing wizards jump quickly.

Not bad. It does have every letter, but it has 31 letters altogether, so some of the letters are being used more than once. This next one has only 26 letters, but it cheats a bit, by using an abbreviation and an unusual spelling:

Blowzy night-frumps vex'd Jack Q.

If you do decide to have a go, you'll find words like *veldt* and *quiz* very useful, as well as words spelled without a normal vowel (*a, e, i, o, u*), such as *fly, cwm,* and *glyph.* And don't forget your dictionary. You'll need a big one!

 word games

paragraph (**pa**-ruh-grahf)

Probably for as long as you can remember, teachers have been telling you to 'start a new paragraph'. Why do they keep going on about it? It's quite simple, really. If you don't break up your written work into smaller chunks, it becomes very difficult to read, and the ideas can get so muddled up that people won't be able to understand what you're trying to say. So, if you want to be clearly understood, use **paragraphs**. (If you don't, then go boil an egg.)

Now, I'm about to make a new point, so I'm starting a new paragraph. That's the main reason for having them, after all. Each new paragraph tells your reader that you're about to say something different. That's why the paragraph stands out so much on the page. The opening line usually starts a little way in (see the entry on **indentation** to find out about this), and there's usually some space after the last sentence as well. In some styles of writing (such as in this book), new paragraphs are separated in a different way – by leaving a space above and below.

Here's a good example of the way you can mix people up, if you don't divide your writing correctly into paragraphs. Imagine I'm writing a news report for the radio. Can you tell where I've made a mistake, and should have started a new paragraph?

In Washington this morning, President Bush met the Soviet leader Mr Gorbachev for talks. After the meeting, both leaders issued a joint statement expressing their concern for peace. In London, a panda has given birth to twins. Both mother and babies are doing well.

I hope the news-reader spots it in time!

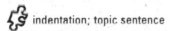 indentation; topic sentence   discourse; text

paraphrase (**pa**-ruh-frayz)

I'd be grateful if you would depart directly.
I'd like you to leave straight away.
I want you to 'op it now!

These three messages tell the same story, more or less. They're very different in style, of course – the first is very formal and polite, the third is very informal and rude. But they basically say the same thing. When one sentence has the same meaning as another, we say that the two sentences are **paraphrases** of each other. Here's another example:

The fat dog chased the skinny cat.
The skinny cat was chased by the fat dog.

These two sentences mean exactly the same thing. The second sentence is a paraphrase of the first, and the first sentence is a paraphrase of the second.

You can have paraphrases of bigger pieces of language, too. Has a teacher ever said to you, 'Read this, then write it down in your own words'? (No groaning!) What you're going to come up with is a paraphrase. Why do teachers do this sort of thing? Well, it's a good way of checking that you've clearly understood what you've been reading. And it's a good way of training you to write briefly and precisely. It can be hard work and a bit boring at times, I admit. But then, so is training for the Olympics.

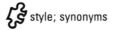 style; synonyms

parentheses see **brackets**

parts of speech

Next time you feel like having a nightmare, try this. You're in a room, surrounded by all the words in English – hundreds of thousands of them. A monster says you have to sort all the words out into their different kinds, or he'll bite your head off. What will you do – apart from wake up? Actually, there's no need to lose your head. It's not so difficult. All you have to do is take some sentences, and see which words fit into which places. Like this:

He can see a big pig.

Now, how many words can you find that can go in place of *pig*? There are thousands, so I'll just give you five: *castle*, *cup*, *fish*, *mountain*, and *lighthouse*. Words of this kind are usually called **nouns**. Next, find some words that can go in place of *see*. Again, there are thousands, so here's another five: *kick*, *cook*, *eat*, *love*, and *sell*. These words are usually called **verbs**. The words that replace *can* are verbs, too – but of a rather different kind (see the entry on **auxiliary verb**, to find out more about them). Next, if you replace *big* by *fat*, *happy*, *large*, and other such words, you'll end up with the grouping called **adjectives**. There are thousands of adjectives in English. Now look for words that could go in place of *he*. Only a small number, this time: *I*, *you*, *she*, *we*, and a few others. They're called **pronouns**. The words that can replace *a* are also very few *the*, *that*, *my*, and so on. These are called **determiners**, and the chief determiners – *the* and *a* – are called **articles**.

When you group words into types, like this, the groupings you end up with are called the **parts of speech**. (Actually, this term is a bit misleading, as the same groupings are found in writing as well as in speech, so linguists often use the term **word classes** instead.) This entry hasn't mentioned all the parts of speech yet. To discover **prepositions**, **conjunctions**, and **adverbs**, you'd need to take a different kind of sentence. But I'm sure I've given you enough examples to prove that you can solve your nightmare problem. If you want to know more, the main parts of speech in English are each given a separate entry in this book.

 grammar

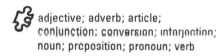 adjective; adverb; article; conjunction; conversion; interjection; noun; preposition; pronoun; verb

 determiner

past tense

Who said, 'I came, I saw, I conquered'?
Julius Caesar, talking about his visit to
Britain. He was talking about what
happened some time before, so his verbs
had to be in the **past tense**. Most verbs in
English form their past tense in a very
simple way, by adding an *-ed* ending. *I
jump – I jumped. I walk – I walked. I call – I
called. I knit – I knitted.* (Notice that in
speech, these endings are pronounced
differently. In *walked*, the *-ed* sounds like
the *t* in *cat*. In *called*, it sounds like the *d* in
old. And in *knitted*, it sounds like the *id* in
did.) However, there are a large number of
verbs which don't form their past tense in
this way, and these are called the **irregular
verbs**. Here are some irregular past tenses,
with the present tense form in brackets:

took (take) *went* (go) *put* (put)
caught (catch) *did* (do) *was* (is)

It's quite a job, learning the irregular verbs
in English, as any foreigner will tell you.
And if you've had to learn irregular verbs
in French or German, you're probably
thinking, 'Serves them right!'

 tense; verb

pen name see **pseudonym**

period see **full stop**

periphrasis see **circumlocution**

person

Think of an action. Eating? (I might have guessed!) All right. Now,
who's doing the eating? English gives us three ways of saying who's

doing what, when people talk to each other. First of all, it might be the speaker who is eating. If it is, the sentence would have to be something like this: *I am eating my lunch*. If it is the listener who is eating, the sentence would have to be different: *You are eating your lunch*. And if it's neither the speaker nor the listener eating, but a spotty youth on the next table, the sentence would have to be different again: *He is eating his lunch*. The pronouns *I*, *you*, and *he* are here referring to the different kinds of people, or **persons**, involved. There are three kinds:

- The pronouns which refer to the **first person** – the person who is speaking or writing – are *I*, *me*, *my*, *mine*, and *myself*. *We*, *us*, *our*, *ours*, and *ourselves* are used if the speaker joins in with others: *We are eating our lunch*.
- The pronouns which refer to the **second person** – the person or persons you're talking or writing to – are *you*, *your*, *yours*, *yourself*, and *yourselves*.
- The pronouns which refer to the **third person** – the person or persons you're talking about – are *he*, *she*, *it*, *they*, and similar words (*him*, *herself*, *theirs*, and so on).

GOVERNMENT WORD WARNING! The term 'person' doesn't just refer to human beings. You can talk to an animal in the second person (*Are you hungry?*) or even an object (*You stupid typewriter!*). In the same way, you can use the third person to refer to animals, places, things, ideas, or anything. *It's under the stairs. They're lovely countries. She's a ferocious beast!*

 pronoun number

personal pronoun see **pronoun**

personification (per-son-if-i-**kay**-shuhn)

Oh, isn't she absolutely gorgeous!

What is this speaker talking about? If it's a lady or a female animal, this is a perfectly normal way of using the feminine pronoun *she*. But what if it's something that isn't a person or an animal? What if the speaker was pointing to a yacht, or a car, or a vacuum cleaner? (Why not? Some vacuum cleaners look lovely!) These would be cases of **personification** – giving an object human qualities. Countries are often thought of as feminine, also. People say things like *England needs to look after her national parks*. I call my word

processor *Alfie*, and talk about him in masculine terms. But it's not just pronouns which make you think of objects as human. You can use any words which would normally be used of people. Here's a line of poetry I just made up, about someone visiting Snowdon:

The mountain smiled, and seemed to welcome me.

Mountains don't smile and welcome. People do that. But I'm sure you can still make sense of the line.

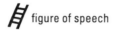 figure of speech   metaphor   ² impersonal style; metonymy

phrase

Dogs chew bones noisily.

This isn't a scientific discovery. It's just an example of a simple four-part sentence. What's doing the action? Dogs. What are the dogs doing? Chewing. What are they chewing? Bones. How do they chew their bones? Noisily. Each part, or element, of the sentence is just one word long. Nice and simple. However, most sentences aren't like this. Usually, the different parts contain *more* than one word. Like this:

Bones? What sort of bones?
Tasty bones. Large tasty bones. Large tasty bones with meat on.

Or this:

Noisily? How noisily?
Very noisily. Very very noisily. Very very very noisily.

Or this:

Dogs? Which dogs?
My dogs. John's dogs. Those dogs. My three long-haired dogs.
Those horrible big cross-eyed dogs from next door.

The point is: they all chew bones noisily.

Whenever a group of words works together as a single element in a sentence, it's called a **phrase**. There are several different kinds of phrase, depending on which of the words is thought to be the chief one (you can look some of them up, using the list at the end of this entry). But beware! In a sentence, it's sometimes difficult to tell what the phrases are. The easiest test is to see whether you can replace a group of words by a single word. Here's an example:

The fat frog   was croaking   in the garden   at midnight.
  He   *croaked*   *there*   *then.*

There are four phrases in this sentence. How many are there in this one?

Two more frogs were croaking outside at three o'clock.

Only three, this time. *Outside* isn't a phrase. (Did you try the test? 'They croaked outside then.')

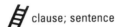 clause; sentence   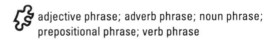 adjective phrase; adverb phrase; noun phrase; prepositional phrase; verb phrase

plural see **number**

positive see **affirmative** and **negative**

predicate (**pred**-i-kuht)

What's the best way of dividing a sentence into two parts? You could, I suppose, take a ruler, and measure exactly half way through. Let's see how that would work:

My mum spoke to Charlie in the street.

This sentence has got 30 letters in it, so half way through would be right in the middle of *Charlie*. Painful. There must be a better way of starting off the study of the structure of a sentence. And there is. You look for two points. First, ask, 'Who or what is the sentence about?' 'What's the *topic* of the sentence?' Then ask, 'And what is being said about this topic?' Here's an easy example:

My model boat has crashed.

What's the sentence about? My model boat. And what's happened to the model boat? It's crashed. Now try it this way:

My model boat has crashed into the end of the pool.

A much longer sentence this time, but the two questions have the same answers. What's the sentence about? My model boat. And what's happened to it? It's crashed into the end of the pool. Putting this another way, *my model boat* is called the **subject** of the sentence (look up the entry on **subject**, to find out more about this), and everything else is called the **predicate**. The predicate includes the verb, and anything else after the verb. So, can you find the predicate in the *Charlie* sentence at the top of this entry? (It's everything except *my mum*.)

By the way, don't expect all sentences to have the structure of a subject and a predicate. *Hello* doesn't, for instance. Nor does *Sit down* or *Lovely day* or *Out of order*. But if it were *Tuesday was a lovely day* or *My phone is out of order*, that would be different.

 sentence   subject

prefix see **affix**

preposition (pre-puh-**zi**-shuhn)

Is my homework in the fridge?
Is my homework by the fridge?
Is my homework under the fridge?
Is my homework behind the fridge?

All right. I can see you've lost your homework. But before you go searching, let's just look at those sentences. Each sentence is about homework and a fridge, but they mean different things. The homework is in different places, thanks to the words *in*, *by*, *under*, and *behind*. These words are some of the **prepositions** in English. They're called prepositions because they go in 'pre' position. Does that help? Well, it will if I tell you that 'pre' is from Latin, and means 'in front of'. Prepositions go in front of certain other words – most often, in front of nouns and noun phrases. They're very important words, because they show you how these nouns relate to each other in space and time. If you get the preposition wrong, it can be very misleading. Is Fred *in* his car, or *under* his car? Is the meeting *before* three o'clock, *at* three o'clock, or *after* three o'clock? Did the striker kick the ball *into* the goal, *above* the goal, or *behind* the goal? There are dozens of prepositions, in fact, and they express a wide range of meanings. For instance, as well as space and time, they can tell you about the cause of something or the way something was done. Look at these:

The burglar opened the lock **with** his teeth.
My hair's soaked **because** of the rain.

There are other meanings, too. But have you noticed something important about this last sentence? The preposition *because of* has got two words in it. That's fine. Don't panic. There are lots of prepositions like that – such as *up to*, *out of*, and *together with*. You can even have some rather special prepositions with three or more words, such as *in place of* and *on top of*. There! Your homework was on top of the fridge all the time.

 noun; noun phrase; parts of speech

prepositional phrase

prepositional phrase

Do you remember the saga of the lost homework (read the entry on **preposition**, if you don't)? Read All About It! Homework Found On Fridge! Did you notice that there was a very close link between the prepositions and the noun phrases which followed them? The prepositions seemed to stick to the noun phrases. If I start to move things round the sentence, you'll see what I mean.

My homework was on the fridge.
On the fridge I found my homework.
It was on the fridge that I found my homework.

Do you see what happens? Wherever I put *the fridge, on* goes too. *On the fridge* is a type of phrase. (You can check that it's a phrase, because you can replace *on the fridge* by a single word, if you want, such as *there*. Try it.) So, what sort of a phrase is it? It's a **prepositional phrase**, because the leading word is a preposition. I think that's all I need to say, for the moment – except to give you a few other examples of prepositional phrases to finish off this entry. How do you feel about that? Under the weather? In good spirits? Over the moon? Sick – as a parrot?

phrase; preposition

present tense

Darling, I love you terribly, I'm thinking of you every moment. I want to be near you. I want to hold your hand. I want –

All right, that's enough of that. Let's get on with some grammar. Love letters use a lot of verbs in this way: *I want, I love, I'm thinking*. So do sports commentaries:

Smith is running down the wing. He picks up the ball, and passes it to Jones. Jones is looking for Brown, and he finds him. Brown shoots –

Only a grammarian would turn the radio off at that point! I've collected enough verbs, though: *is running*, *picks up*, *passes*, *finds*, *shoots*. So, what have all these verbs got in common? They're all in the **present tense**. They all say what's happening *now*, in the present, at the moment of speaking or writing. While I write this letter, I *am feeling* my love for you. While I talk, Smith *is kicking* the ball. Sounds simple enough. The present tense form of the verb tells you about present time. That's the way it usually is. But unfortunately (you're going to love this), the present tense can tell you about future and past time, too. If you use it with a future adverb, such as *tomorrow*, it doesn't refer to the present any more: *Mike is going to France tomorrow*. Even though the present tense is used (*is going*), this sentence certainly doesn't mean that Mike is travelling now! And here's an example of the present tense being used to refer to a time in the past:

READ ALL ABOUT IT! MINISTER DIES!

Does this mean that the minister is dying at the moment you read the headline? Not a bit. The minister died yesterday. It's over. But the newspaper still uses the present tense, to keep the drama going.

 tense; verb    future tense; past tense

progressive or continuous

DON: What happened at the meeting?
RON: I asked one question, then I went home.
DON: What about Dick?
RON: Humph! *He* was asking questions all evening!

When an action goes on for a long time, it's usual to talk about it using a two-part verb. The first part is a word like *is* or *was* (see the entry on **auxiliary verb**, for more about these). The second part is a verb with an *-ing* ending. So, we have *He was asking*, *John was sneezing*, *The car is stopping*, and many more. The main use of this verb form is to emphasise the length of the action. It tells you that an action is (or was, or will be) in progress over a period of time. So it's called the **progressive** or **continuous** form of the verb. If you don't use this form, your only other choice is to use the verb in its **simple** form, as in *He asked*, *John sneezed*, and *The car stops*. The simple form has many uses, but you'll often find that it doesn't give quite so much emphasis to the idea of an action continuing over a period of time. Here are the two forms, side by side:

Simple
Eric dropped the ball.

Progressive
Eric was dropping the ball.

Do you feel the different senses? The simple form tells you that Eric dropped the ball, and that's it. The progressive form tells you that he kept on doing it. You can bring out the difference more clearly if you add some extra time words, like this:

Eric dropped the ball just once.
Eric was dropping the ball all through the game.

It would sound odd to say *Eric was dropping the ball just once*!

GOVERNMENT WORD WARNING! Not all verbs in English can be used in the progressive form. We don't usually say **I am knowing the answer* or **I am liking this ice cream* or **I am owning a new bike*.

 verb   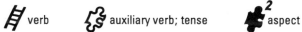 auxiliary verb; tense   aspect

pronoun (**proh**-nown)

What's wrong with this way of writing?

The little old lady in a raincoat walked into the shop. The little old lady in a raincoat asked for a pint of milk. The shopkeeper gave the little old lady in a raincoat the milk and asked the little old lady in a raincoat if the little old lady in a raincoat wanted anything else.

I imagine you'd prefer it to be like this:

The little old lady in a raincoat walked into the shop. She asked for a pint of milk. The shopkeeper gave her the milk and asked her if she wanted anything else.

She is a useful little word, isn't it? It saves you having to repeat that long noun phrase (*the little old lady in a raincoat*) every time. It stands in for the noun phrase. In Latin, the word for 'for' is *pro*, so when grammarians invented the name for words like *she*, they called them 'pro-nouns' – words which stand in 'for nouns'. There are several different sorts of **pronoun** in English. *He* is an example of a **personal pronoun**, because it refers to a person. The personal pronouns in English are *I* and *me*, *you*, *he* and *him*, *she* and *her*, *we* and *us*, *they* and

them – and *it* is brought in as well, even though it doesn't (usually) refer to people. Pronouns do all kinds of jobs. Some, such as *my* and *hers*, tell you who owns something. Some, such as *all* and *some*, tell you how much of something there is. Some, such as *this* and *that*, tell you how near something is to you. Here are a few examples:

These are *mine*. Do *you* want *some*? *That's* a nice *one*.

Of course, until I give you a noun or two, these sentences won't mean very much. Let's imagine it's Joan Jones talking about apples to Will Williams. Now they make sense.

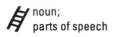 noun; parts of speech   gender    antecedent; demonstrative; indefinite pronoun; interrogative; reflexive pronoun; relative

proper noun and common noun

These are the two main kinds of noun. The **proper nouns** are easy to spot, because they're written with a capital letter at the beginning. They're also called **proper names**, because they name particular people, places, days, months, festivals, magazines, comics, films, and so on. Here is a short collection, taken from the newspaper I was reading this morning:

London   The Independent   October   Kuwait
Margaret Thatcher   Mr Bush

Common nouns are all the others. Most of the nouns in this entry are common nouns. Look at my third sentence, for instance – the one beginning 'They're also called'. That's got a good collection of common nouns in it.

What's the main difference between a proper noun and a common noun? A proper noun refers to something that's the only one of its kind. There's just one city of London, one month called October, one Margaret Thatcher. And as a result, we don't usually put these nouns into the plural and say *Kuwaits, Londons, Margaret Thatchers,* or *Octobers*. Common nouns are called 'common' because the nouns refer to common things and ideas which turn up everywhere. *Table, cat, dancer,* and *mud* are all common nouns. Each of these nouns stands for a vast number of things. Any cat which could exist is referred to by the noun *cat*. But *Twiddles* is a particular cat, living at Number 33 – so *Twiddles* is a proper noun.

 noun   upper case

proverb (**pro**-verb)

Too many cooks spoil the broth.
There's no smoke without fire.
A fool and his money are soon parted.
The early bird catches the worm.
One good turn deserves another.

These are all **proverbs** – wise sayings, passed on down the years. They say something that people widely believe – some kind of everyday truth. They're always short sentences, often with a catchy rhythm. Many of them have got two parts, which balance each other:

Least said, soonest mended.
Waste not, want not.
Spare the rod, and spoil the child.
Once bitten, twice shy.

You have to be very careful with proverbs. They don't always mean what they seem to mean. For instance, *Too many cooks spoil the broth* isn't just a proverb about how things might go wrong in the kitchen. You could say this whenever *any* group of people are trying to do *any* kind of job, and getting in each other's way.

It's interesting to collect proverbs. Here are two of my favourites, which I found in a book of old country sayings:

Better a wet mitten than a cold hand.
Save your wind to cool your porridge.

 figure of speech; idiom; metaphor   aphorism

pseudonym (**syoo**-duh-nim)

This is the Greek word for 'false name'. If you're writing something, and you don't want to use your real name, you can call yourself something else instead, and this is your **pseudonym** or **pen name**. Why would you ever want to do such a thing? It might be simply because you don't like your real name, and think a different name would sound better. If you've just written a really romantic love story, and your name is Bill Bloggins, your publisher might well suggest that you change it to something like Malcolm Freshwater – or even change sex, and call yourself Amanda Faithful! A more serious reason for using a pseudonym is to let you hide behind it –

especially if you're writing something that could get you into trouble. I bet if you wrote a note to the headteacher saying 'Down With School!' you wouldn't sign it with your real name! Pseudonyms can be very useful. And some very famous people have used them. Do you know who Boz was? It was the name Charles Dickens used for a while. And have you read any stories by Charles Lutwidge Dodgson? I'm sure you have – but he called himself Lewis Carroll, when he wrote *Alice in Wonderland*.

pun

ANNOYING CHILD: Must I go to the church fete, mum?
MOTHER: Yes. No arguments.
ANNOYING CHILD: But it's going to be a 'fete' worse than death.

Don't groan. You've cracked far worse jokes – if you can call them jokes! What we've got here is a play on words – a kind of practical joke, using language. They're known as **puns**. Some people hate them. Some love them. But you can't get away from them. You'll find them on T-shirts, car stickers, advertisements, newspaper headlines – and all over the walls. Here's one I saw last week. A large poster outside a church said: WHO IS MY NEIGHBOUR? Underneath, someone had written: *Unfortunately yes, Signed The Daleks*.

 word games

punctuation (puhngk-tyoo-**ay**-shuhn)

What else can you see on the pages of this book, apart from the letters? A lot of white space. Some cartoons. A few numbers and special symbols, such as and ♯ . But mainly, there are all the **punctuation marks**. So far in this entry, I have used several kinds of punctuation: a question mark, a full stop, some commas, and a capital letter at the beginning of each sentence – as well as the spaces between words. And now I've just used a dash. And an apostrophe. There aren't many more punctuation marks left: there's the colon, of course; and the semi-colon; and the hyphen; and the use of inverted commas for quoting speech and a few other 'special' cases. Have I shown you a question mark or an exclamation mark yet? No. I mean yes! (I mustn't forget about brackets, either.) There are a few other minor punctuation marks, too, but maybe some other time . . .

Why do we have punctuation marks at all? They do three jobs. One job is to keep pieces of language separate from each other: for instance, spaces keep words apart, and full stops help to keep sentences apart. Another job is to show the beginning and end of something: for instance, one inverted comma marks the beginning of what someone is saying, and the other inverted comma marks the end. The third job is to tell you what sort of word or sentence you're reading: for instance, a question mark tells you that you're reading a question; an apostrophe can tell you that a letter has been left out, as part of informal writing (as in *it's*).

withoutpunctuationithinkthatsentenceswould getverydifficulttoread

 apostrophe; brackets; colon; comma; dash; exclamation; full stop; hyphen; inverted commas; question; semi-colon; upper case

question

MANJIT: Yes, it is.
RANJIT: Is it true that you know what someone's going to say next?

The point of this piece of madness is that it shows you how questions normally work. A **question** is a sentence which usually expects a response. Different kinds of question get different kinds of response. There are three main types, all signalled in writing by the use of a special punctuation mark, the **question mark**.

● A *yes-no* **question** is one where you can give the response 'yes' or 'no'. *Do you like chips? Is your mum in?*

● A *wh-***question** (say it as separate letters, *w h*) is one beginning with a special question word, such as *what, why, when, who, where,* and *how*. They're called *wh-*

questions because most of these words begin with the letters *w* + *h*. They're very different from *yes-no* questions: you have to give them a detailed answer. *Where's Freddy? What's that called?*

● An **alternative question** gives you a choice of answers. You choose one of the alternatives given in the question. *Do you want tea or coffee? Will he be here on Monday or on Tuesday?*

By the way, you can answer a question by another question, if you want.

RANJIT: Are you going to watch TV?
MANJIT: What do *you* think?

You can also ask a question which you answer yourself. Shall I give you an example? Yes, I shall. And you can even ask a question which you don't expect anyone to answer at all. But I'm not sure whether I should give you an example of that. Do you think I'm crazy?

 sentence   command; exclamation; statement   inversion; interrogative

quotation marks see **inverted commas**

rebus (**ree**-buhs)

Translate this:

I c u R 2 YY 4 me 2 catch u out.

'I see you are too wise for me to catch you out.' Easy? All right, try this one:

I had fecantion, so I night in ground.

Got it yet? It reads: 'I had an infection, so I stayed overnight in the underground.' How does it work? Well, 'fecantion' is the word *an* inside the word *fection – an* in *fection*! There's a great game, called

Dingbats, which gives you hundreds of puzzles like this. They're called rebuses. A **rebus** is a word game which uses pictures, numbers, or single letters of the alphabet to make up words and sentences. In children's comics and puzzle books, you'll often see rebuses with pictures in place of words – a picture of a bee instead of the word *be*, for instance. They're great fun to make up.

 word games

regional dialect see **dialect**

register see **variety**

relevance (**rel**-uh-vuhns)

MEG: What's the best way of getting from Liverpool to Newcastle?
GREG: Oh yes, I can tell you that. You have to go to Manchester, where I stayed a couple of weeks ago, as a matter of fact. And I met Fred there – you remember Fred? – he was going to a meeting, so we spent an evening together in a pub just off the High Street. Wasn't that interesting?
MEG: Yes, but how do I get from Liverpool to Newcastle?

What Greg said may indeed have been interesting, but it certainly didn't keep to the point. His answer wandered off in all directions. Keeping to the point is called **relevance**. Going away from the point is called **irrelevance**. It's usually quite easy to spot when someone else is being irrelevant. You feel puzzled and irritated. 'What's that got to do with it?', you say to yourself. But it's much more difficult to stop *yourself* being irrelevant, when you're talking or writing. If it's a complicated piece of writing, such as an essay or a story, then you'd do well to read it through carefully, to check. I do. After I finish this entry, I'll read it over several times to check that everything I've said is relevant to the idea of relevance. If I've put something in that's irrelevant, I'll cut it out. But you'll never know what it was, of course, because by the time you read this entry, it's long gone!

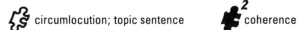 circumlocution; topic sentence   coherence

reported speech see **direct speech**

rhyme (riem)

Jack and Jill went up the hill, to fetch a pail of water.
Jack fell down, and broke his crown, but then got up and caught her.

Well, it rhymes better than the original line, I think: 'and Jill came tumbling after'. I've never thought that *water* and *after* made a particularly good rhyme. But *water* and *caught her* go well together. Or perhaps I should try to make a line up ending with *daughter*, *fought her*, *quarter*, or *taught her*. You try (I can't just now, because I've got the rest of this entry to write). We usually talk about **rhyme** when lines of poetry sound the same at the end. The rhyme might be just one beat of rhythm long (*bug* and *jug*), or two beats (*water* and *daughter*), or three beats (*battery* and *cattery*), or even more. Also, you can get *patterns* of rhyme in a poem. Sometimes the first line rhymes with the third, and the second with the fourth. Sometimes, the lines rhyme in pairs. And there are lots of other possibilities.

By the way, you'll also find rhyming in other places apart from poetry. It's unusual to have it in everyday conversation – and when you do, you often feel you have to apologise for it ('Coo! I've been a poet, and I didn't know it!') But you'll often hear it in slogans for TV commercials, for instance. How's about 'You'll brush all right with Tootheebright'? And you might even find it in essay writers who are trying to be clever. Such as me? Never.

🧩 metre; rhythm   🧩² alliteration; assonance; eye rhyme

(Shakespeare gets angry)

Forsooth, you've made your mother mad;
But don't dare try it on your dad.
You think a whacking will make me sad;
Forget it, son—
it'll make me glad!

rhythm

You'll all know about rhythm in music. Just click those fingers and tap that foot! Well, there's **rhythm** in speech, too. A regular beat. You hear it most clearly in some kinds of poetry. These days, it comes over loud and clear when people rap. Now this little entry's going to have a good beat, While I make my point about rhythm being neat, So prick up your ears and hear what I say, And remember about rhythm in speech, OK? Ahem! Where was I? Ah yes, rhythm in conversation. Even in everyday chat, what you say has a rhythm of loud and soft beats. *I've heard that Jim has got a new bike*. Tap it out, using 'tum' for a loud beat, and 'te' for a soft beat. It'll go like this: 'te-**tum**-te-**tum**-te-**tum**-te-te-**tum**'. Of course, conversational rhythms aren't as strong and regular as the rhythm in poetry (see the entry on **metre** for more information about that), but there's always some rhythm present. If you watch carefully, when someone's talking, you can often *see* the rhythm, as they nod their head, tap the table, or move their hands up and down in time to the strong beats in their speech. Find some really rhythmic examples, and say them together, like a football crowd does (*We are the champions*!). Everyone's got rhythm!

 metre   stress

110

riddle

I expect you've seen books with names like 'A thousand jokes for kids'? A lot of them are questions like this:

What's yellow, weighs 4 tonnes, and has a blocked trunk?
What's green and hairy and goes up and down?
What do you get if you cross Dracula with a dwarf?

Questions which are deliberately asked so as to puzzle or mislead you are called **riddles**. A riddle describes an object in such a way that you can't see what it is. You have to work it out from the clues given in the description. Children's riddles tend to be short and jokey, with a pun (a play on words) in the answer.

Adult riddles make you think harder, and don't have to be funny. *First I had four legs, then two legs, and now I have three legs. What am I?* Answer: an old man or woman. (Four legs for crawling; two legs for walking; and the third leg is a stick.) If it's a really clever riddle, you feel great when you've guessed the answer, and you kick yourself if you have to be told what it is.

What's that? You want the answers to my three opening riddles? I thought you'd have got them by now. Ah well, here they are. An elephant drowning in a bowl of custard. A gooseberry in a lift. A vampire that bites kneecaps. Satisfied?

 word games   pun

root

Find a complicated word. *Decompression.* Don't worry about what it means. Take it to pieces, by stripping off any bits that have a meaning of their own (see the entry on **affix** to find out more about these). We can take away the *de-*, for instance. That leaves *compression*. Next, get rid of the *-ion*, to leave *compress*. Then remove the *com-*, to leave *press*. Now you've finished. There are no more bits to take away. What you're left with is the **root** or **stem** of the word. The root is the basic identity of a word – the part to which other bits are joined, when you're making bigger words. Here are some other words, with the root in bold type:

going   un**happy**   under**lin**ing (it's **line**, of course, but the spelling hides it)

I don't want to leave you with the impression that all words are complicated ones, though. A very large number consist of just a root, and nothing else – words such as *table*, *frog*, and *elephant*, for example. Also, many words consist of *more than one root* – these are the compound words of English, such as *blackbird* and *tugboat*. Compounds are so important that they have an entry of their own.

 word   affix, compound word   morphology

semi-colon (**se**-mee **koh**-luhn)

For breakfast we had the choice of fruit juice or cereal, a boiled, fried, or poached egg, white, brown, or wholemeal bread, and tea or coffee.

Did you find that difficult to read? Look at the bit that says *poached egg, white*, for instance. It's difficult to be sure what *white* is doing in the sentence. You have to read the whole thing a couple of times before you can work out which words belong together. The problem, of course, is that the sentence is badly punctuated. Whoever wrote it didn't know much about punctuation. The writer has tried to make the comma do all the hard work of organising the sentence, and the poor old comma just can't cope. What the writer should have done is bring in the cavalry, in the form of the **semi-colon**. This is what the same sentence would look like with

some semi-colons in:

For breakfast we had the choice of fruit juice or cereal; a boiled, fried, or poached egg; white, brown, or wholemeal bread; and tea or coffee.

Do you see how the semi-colon is used? It shows you what the main parts of the sentence are when you're stringing together a set of lengthy points. Within each part, you can carry on using commas, if you have to – but now there's no muddle. Semi-colons are most helpful when you've got a lot of very complex pieces of language to string together, so you're more likely going to find them used in formal writing, such as textbooks. You won't find very many in the book you're reading now.

 comma; punctuation   colon

sentence

The police burst into the room. Murphy lay on the settee, his chest covered with blood. Branson went over to him. There was very little time. 'Who did it, Murphy?' Branson put his ear next to the dying man's lips. 'Who did it?' Murphy's eyes flickered. 'It was . . . It was . . .' His head fell back. Branson cursed. Their last lead had gone.

Branson's problem was that Murphy didn't finish his sentence – though poor old Murphy didn't really have much choice in the matter!

It's sometimes quite easy to recognise a sentence. In writing, most of the time, all you need to do is look out for a capital letter at the beginning of a piece of writing, and a certain type of punctuation mark at the end – usually a full stop (.), a question mark (?), or an exclamation mark (!). If the sentence isn't finished, you'll find the writer uses different punctuation, such as a dash (–) or dots (. . .), as in the extract above.

Did you notice I said 'most of the time' just now? That's because sometimes, in the written language, you find sentences that *don't* end with a punctuation mark. Look at the notices and signs around the school, or record labels, or shop signs, or posters and advertisements. If someone writes a poster in large capital letters saying SPECIAL MEETING TODAY, there probably won't be a full stop at the end. (Sometimes, advertisements have sentences which don't begin with a capital letter, either. Keep an eye out for them. They're rather special.) It can also be quite difficult to recognise a sentence in speech, where of course there are no capital letters or full stops, and you have to listen to the melody of the voice, the rhythm, and the pauses to know when a sentence has come to an end.

So, what is a **sentence**? There are three chief things to look out for.

• A sentence can stand on its own. It doesn't have to lean on any other bit of language in order to sound finished. So, *Because I haven't got any money* couldn't be a sentence. It needs something else to finish it off (such as *I couldn't lend him 5p*).

- Only certain combinations of words can be sentences. *The cat's being sick* is an unfortunate fact, but it makes an excellent English sentence. **Sick the being's cat* doesn't. You have to follow the rules of the language.
- You can see from this that a sentence usually makes sense. *The cat's being sick* is a sentence. *The* isn't. Nor is *cat's, being, the cat's,* or any other combination of these words. These bits just don't make sense. But beware! You can sometimes find a sentence that follows all the rules, but it makes no sense at all. Have you read Lewis Carroll's *Jabberwocky*? He uses such sentences as *'Twas brillig, and the slithy toves did gyre and gimble in the wabe*. They're splendid sentences, though complete nonsense.

When you study the structure of sentences, to find out which word combinations are possible, and which aren't, you're studying the **grammar** of the language. You'll come across the word **sentence** many times in this book. When you learn a language, you learn to speak and write the sentences of that language. And when you learn *about* a language (which is what you're doing now), you learn – more than anything else – about the structure of its sentences.

 grammar

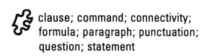 clause; command; connectivity; formula; paragraph; punctuation; question; statement

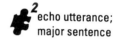 echo utterance; major sentence

simile (**si**-mi-lee)

Here are some of the ways famous authors have talked about trees:

A pear tree glistened like a graceful drift of snow . . .
The branches looked like the fingers of a gigantic hand . . .
Evergreens as big as tents . . .
Maples, burning like bonfires, pure yellow and pure red . . .
The poplars stood like tall guards, at attention . . .
Rows of bay trees like children's green lollipops . . .
The trees drooped like old men with back problems . . .

Good stuff, eh? My favourite is the last one. So, how shall we talk about the language here? The writers have been comparing the trees to something else. When you do this, and show that you're doing it by using a special 'comparing' word – usually *like* or *as* – it's called a *simile*. You can make up your own similes, if you want. Have a simile competition. Someone starts a sentence off, and stops at *like*.

Each entrant finishes off the sentence, and then you judge which was the funniest, or the most vivid, or whatever. Try this one:

After the Christmas play, the infants' classroom looked like –

A battlefield? A line of washing after a tornado? Now your turn.

 figure of speech   imagery, metaphor

singular see **number**

slang

TOUGH LOUT: Hey, cop this, scribbler. Stop taking the mick out of me mates or I'll duff yer up.
ME: Who, me? I'm sorry, but I think you must be talking to the wrong person. I haven't been taking the mick – I beg your pardon, making fun of any of your friends, so there certainly won't be any need to attack me. Anyway, my bro's a bouncer, so watch your own mug, savvy?

Good, he's gone. It's useful being a linguist, sometimes. Right, let's get on. This little conversation shows some of the very informal words and phrases we use which aren't part of the standard language. This kind of speech is called **slang**. It's used by everyone, at some time or other, but it's especially common among young people. You'll also find a lot of slang among special groups. Sailors, the police, cricketers, artists, carpenters, computer scientists, criminals . . . they all have their slang. Sometimes, the language is so unusual that it's not possible to work out what the people are talking about. The most famous case of this is the **rhyming slang** used by Cockney traders in London – *apples and pears* for stairs, *artful dodger* for a lodger, *cherry ripe* for a pipe, and *mince*

pies for eyes. It would take you quite a while to work out what this sentence means, for instance: *Old Fred left 'is Humpstead Heath in the lean and lurch.* Or in other words: 'Old Fred left his teeth in the church'.

Why do people use slang? Well, you know what they say:

I use slang
To show I'm one of the gang.

It's a good point. When people use slang among themselves, it shows that they belong together. The slang marks them out as being members of the same group – just like a uniform would. It shows that they're different from everyone else. There'll be lots of slang in the streets where you live. Keep an ear open for it, and see if it tells you anything about the groups the people belong to. And don't forget school. First-year slang won't always be the same as third-year or fifth-year slang. And even teachers have their own slang, too!

formal; standard English

colloquial speech, style; variety   argot

115

slogan (**sloh**-guhn)

Have you or your family ever entered a magazine competition to win a splendid car or to go on a month's holiday in Florida? I don't expect you won. The problem is often not the questions they ask, but the piece of writing you have to make up at the end. 'Say in not more than ten words why your cat should eat Nuglits.' What the magazine wants is a catchy phrase which will say something good about – well, Nuglits, in this case. It wants a **slogan**. How's about *No Nuglits is a no-no for puss-puss*? (I should say that I've never won a slogan competition either.) Here are a few famous slogans from the advertising world in recent years:

Drinka Pinta Milka Day.
Beanz Meanz Heinz.
Heineken refreshes the parts other beers cannot reach.
Know about language, for lifelong life-support.

What's that? You don't remember the last one? You will.

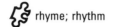 rhyme; rhythm   alliteration

I never win at competitions because.....

speech marks see **inverted commas**

116

spoonerism (**spoo**-nuh-ri-zuhm)

Everyone gets a slip of the tongue, from time to time. You intend to say one thing, and something else comes out. Instead of saying *My mum's baked a cake*, you say *My mum's caked a bake*! A sound from one word swops with a sound from another word. Something's gone temporarily wrong with the programming of our personal computer (our brain, I mean). Often people hardly realise they've made an error, but sometimes the change in the sounds produces a completely different meaning which stands out a mile. When a tongue-slip is very noticeable like this, we call it a **spoonerism**. Why? Because of the

famous slips made by one man – William Archibald Spooner (1844–1930), an Anglican clergyman who came to be Warden of New College in Oxford. Apparently, once he got up to speak, and instead of saying *Let us drink to the dear old Queen*, he said *Let us drink to the queer old dean*! And, telling off a student, he is supposed to have said: *You have tasted two whole worms, hissed all my mystery lectures, and been caught fighting a liar in the quad*! I wonder if he really did say this. Or did his students make it up?

 malapropism

standard English

If you went to Australia, and picked up a daily newspaper, you'd be able to read it. The words, the grammar, and the spelling would be hardly any different from the newspapers you can buy in this country. If you went to India, and saw an English-language newspaper there, you'd get the same impression. There'd be a few words and phrases referring to local Indian matters, but on the whole you'd see straight away that the paper was written in the same kind of English as appears in Britain. And in the USA, you'd see the same thing again (apart from a few spelling differences). What you're noticing is the fact that the English language is written in basically the same way all over the English-speaking world. The grammar is largely the same. The vocabulary is largely the same. And the spelling is largely the same. The usage, we can say, is **standard**, and we can describe this international kind of English as **standard English**.

When we speak, there are great similarities all around the world, too. Our accents are very different, of course. You'll always be able to tell an American from a British speaker, for instance (see the entry on **accent**, for more about this). But most of the sound patterns, grammar, and vocabulary will be the same. The idea of a standard English applies to speech, too. If you listen to the radio programmes coming from different English-speaking countries, you'll hear standard English (along with the local accent).

When people *don't* speak or write according to the rules of standard English, you can say that they're using language in a **non-standard** way – it's **non-standard English**. If you disapprove of this way of talking or writing, you can call it, rather more rudely, **sub-standard English**. *I ain't doing nothing* is a good example of a widely used piece of non-standard English. The standard version would be *I'm not doing anything*. *Shut your gob* uses a piece of non-standard vocabulary. Standard English would say *Shut your mouth*. Slang of any kind – the informal words or phrases used by particular groups of people – is a non-standard way of talking. One of the things a school tries to do is teach you to write in standard English, and to speak it (if you don't use it already). It can seem a bit of a bore at times, especially if you're used to talking in a local dialect, and you find it easier to write things down in your homework just as you'd say them with your friends. But that won't help you when, one day, you find you have to write or talk to people in other parts of the country, or other parts of the world. They won't understand you, if you insist on using your local patterns of speech.

 dialect   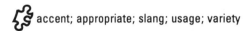 accent; appropriate; slang; usage; variety

statement

This is a book.
You are a reader.
I am giving you some examples of a
  statement.

A **statement** is a kind of sentence whose main job is to give you some information – to 'state' something. It doesn't ask you anything, or tell you to do anything – it just gives you some facts (or some opinions), and you carry on from there. It usually has a subject, and the subject usually goes in front of the verb. In written language, most of the sentences you'll ever read will be statements. Every sentence I'm using in this entry is a statement. Except one. Can you say which one that is?

 sentence; subject; verb   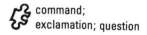 command; exclamation; question

stem see root

118

style

Ben is cycling fast down a hill. He sees his mates and gives them a wave, but loses control of the bike. He starts to fall off, then manages to turn his fall into a somersault, landing on his feet. He keeps the bike going forward, and hops back on, riding off into the sunset as if nothing had happened. 'Man, that's style!', say his mates.

Style in language can be a bit like that. You've got style when you're totally in control of what you're saying or writing. You've got style when you choose the best words to suit your meaning. You've got style when people admire the way you've said something or written something. You've got style when you develop your own personal way of using language, not like anything anyone's ever seen before. People who write novels, plays, and poems all work hard at developing their own style. It doesn't usually come easily. Most people really do have to work hard at it.

You don't have to be famous to have style, though. If you think about it, *everyone*'s got a style. Think of your friends, and how they talk. Have you seen their written work, too? You'll find that each person has a way of using language that belongs to them. And *you*'ve got your own style, therefore – your favourite ways of putting things, your favourite words, the words you *don't* like using, a special tone of voice you often put on . . . Your language style is a mixture of all these things, and it's part of you. It grows and changes as *you* grow and change.

Recognising a style is one thing. Describing it is another. Just think of your favourite TV soap character or comedian. If you heard them talking on the TV in the next room, you'd know straight away who it was. Now, describe exactly what it is in their language which makes you able to do that. Is it their pronunciation, their grammar, or their vocabulary? Is it the way they use nouns, or adjectives, or verbs? One thing's certain. When you try to describe someone's style, you're going to need most of the terms in this book – and more besides.

appropriate; formal; genre; usage; variety

subject (**sub**-jekt)

ME: I'm going to tell you a joke.
YOU: Go on, then.
ME: An Englishman, an Irishman, and a Scotsman –

Now if I stop there, you'll not be pleased. But I have to, I'm afraid, because this is the entry on subjects, and I've just reached the end of the subject of that sentence. The **subject** is the part which tells you what the sentence is going to be about. It sets the theme, or topic, of the sentence. And that's what I've just done. You now know that this sentence is going to be about an Englishman, an Irishman, and a Scotsman. They're the topic of this sentence. If I carried on, I'd have to give you a verb and all sorts of other goodies (see the entry on **predicate** to find out more about that), like this: . . . *were sitting on top of a mountain.*

The subject is often the very first part of the sentence. If I get on with the joke, you'll see this clearly (I'll underline the subjects):

A genie came along and gave them each a wish.
The Englishman wished for a cup of tea.
The Irishman wished for a cup of coffee.
And the Scotsman wished for a glass of whisky.

Of course, if the sentence has more than one clause in it, you may have more than one subject:

When the genie left, the Englishman drank his tea.

If the sentence is quoting what someone said, the subject might be at the very end:

'Funny,' said <u>the Irishman.</u>

And if the sentence is asking a question, the subject will follow the first verb or the question word:

'Why did <u>you</u> say that?', asked <u>the Englishman.</u>

Well, I think that's enough to give you an idea of what subjects are. Sorry. I can't remember the end of the joke. Shall we change the subject?

♯ clause; verb   ⌘ predicate; sentence

subjective case see **case**

subordination (suh-baw di **nay**-shuhn)

Do you know what *subordinate* means? There's a sergeant and a private. Who's the subordinate? Yes, the private. The word basically means 'lower down' or 'in a lower position'. The same basic idea of **subordination** turns up when you're analysing sentences, too. Often, you want to say several things at once, inside a single sentence. How are you going to do it? Let's take the following three points:

Auntie Julie has just been to Africa.
Auntie Flo has just been to Spain.
Auntie Julie has been talking to Auntie Flo.

This is one way of putting everything together:

Auntie Julie, who's just been to Africa, has been talking to Auntie Flo, who's just been to Spain.

There are three clauses in this sentence, but I've chosen one to act as the core of the sentence (the **main clause**). I haven't lost sight of the others, but I'm treating them as less important (they're the **subordinate clauses** or **dependent clauses**). You can see which is the main clause and which are the subordinate clauses if I print them like this:

Main clause   *Auntie Julie   has been talking to Auntie Flo*
Subordinate
    clauses   *who's just been   who's just been*
                           to Africa   to Spain

The word which links the subordinate clause to the main clause is called a **subordinator**. In this sentence, the subordinator is *who* – twice.

In many sentences, the subordinate clause takes up a *whole* element of the main clause. Here's a main clause, containing a subject, a verb, and an object:

I said no!

Now here's the same clause structure, but this time the object is itself a clause:

I said **that Cinderella can't go to the ball**.

And here's an old nursery story which has got a clause inside a clause inside a clause inside a clause inside a clause!!

This is the dog
    that chased the cat
        that killed the rat
            that lived in the house
                that Jack built.

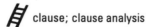 clause; clause analysis   coordination

122

sub-standard English see **standard English**

suffix see **affix**

superlative (soo-**per**-luh-tiv)

I am the greatest. I am the best. I am the most successful fighter in the history of the world.

This isn't me talking. It's Muhammad Ali, when he was at the top of his boxing career. He was known for his superlatives. A **superlative** is the extreme degree that you can have on a scale of meaning. If you can add -*est* to an adjective, you've got a superlative: *greatest*, *biggest*, *tallest*, *tiniest*. And if you can put *most* before an adjective or adverb, you've got a superlative: *most interesting*, *most successfully*. Well, that didn't take long. I wonder if this is the shortest entry in the book?

 degree  comparative

synonyms (**si**-nuh-nimz)
synonymous (si-**no**-ni-muhs)

Bad news, I'm afraid. My pet spider Alfie is dead. Woe is me. He is dead, deceased, passed away, lifeless, departed this life, gone to join his forefathers, gone to the happy hunting grounds . . .

I'm obviously very upset, but I'll control myself for a moment to point out that what we have here is a set of synonyms. **Synonyms** are words or phrases which have the same meaning. So, we have *car* and *automobile*, *help* and *aid*, *blind* and *sightless*, and so on. But beware! Words which may be **synonymous** in one sentence may not be so in another. You go into a shop, and say to yourself, *What a splendid selection of sweets*! *What a splendid range of sweets*! Later you

123

meet a friend, and want to tell him what you saw. Which word will you use – *range* or *selection*? It doesn't much matter. In this situation, the two words are synonyms. But then you look across the bay at the mountains. It's a lovely clear day, so you say *What a splendid mountain range*! However, this time you can't say **What a splendid mountain selection*!

Now, where was I? Oh yes, Alfie is demised, no more, passed over, gone before, six feet under, stone cold, dead as a doornail, in Abraham's bosom, kaput . . .

 antonyms; thesaurus

syntax (**sin**-taks)

No, this is not a tax on sin. (Sorry. That's an ancient joke.) **Syntax** is the main subject studied by English grammar. It's the way words go together to make sentences. The term comes from a Greek word which means 'arrange together'. So, if you look at the first sentence in this entry, syntax studies why the words go in that particular order. Is it possible to change that order in any way? *A tax on sin this is not*. Can you add extra words to it? *This is definitely not a tax on sin*. Can you take words away from it? *This is a tax on sin*. (It's not true, but it's still a grammatical sentence.) What are the impossible ways of changing the sentence around? **A tax sin on this not is*. And are there any problems in the arrangement of the words, which might make people disagree about whether it was a good English sentence or not? I can think of only one: would it have been better to put a full stop after *No*? There's plenty more on syntax in this book, if you go hunting. The cross-references will give you a few leads.

He's just had a tax demond!

Sin Tax

You owe us —

Total

 grammar   clause; coordination; phrase; sentence; subordination    anacoluthon; parsing

taboo word (tuh-**boo**)

I'm really embarrassed about this entry. It's the only one in the book where I can't give you the best examples. They're all taboo, you see. A **taboo word** is one you shouldn't say or write, because people don't like to hear it or read it. Fortunately, I think you'll know a fair number of them, so maybe I can salvage my entry after all. Perhaps all I need do is remind you where you can expect to find taboo words: in relation to religion, death, sex, and going to the toilet. Swear words are the most powerful taboo words. Many people use religious names as swear words, for example. Others either never do this, or water the swear words down so that they sound different – saying *Gosh!* instead of *God!* for instance. In writing, taboo words would, in the past, never be used – or at best would be printed using dashes, like this: *that b– – – – –fool!* Today, novels and plays often print these words in full, and in the later part of the evening you'll regularly hear them on radio and television. But if I were to print a word like *bloody* in full in a schoolbook, I can't imagine what parents would say. So I won't.

 euphemism expletive

telegrammatic speech (te-li-gruh-**ma**-tik)

Come home quick. Hamster ill. Vet worried. Love Mum.

This is the kind of language people used to use when sending a telegram. You had to pay for every word used, you see, so people left out all the little words, and just put the important ones in. People don't send telegrams much now, but the style is still sometimes used in writing where you have to 'pay by the word' (for instance, when you send an ad to a newspaper). However, the term at the top of this entry is **telegrammatic speech**, not 'telegrammatic writing'. Who would ever speak remotely like this? The answer is: young children in the early stages of learning sentence structure. Here's a range of sentences used by a two-year-old I know:

Daddy gone car.   Where bike?   Where mummy gone?   Car all-gone.

A little later, this child started to put in some of the 'little' words, such as *the* and *is* – but it took a year before she was able to use all these words well. The telegrammatic stage – also called the **telegraphic** stage – in children's speech lasts quite a while.

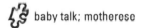 baby talk; motherese holophrase

tense

When you look verbs up in a dictionary, they don't seem to do very much – *go, come, jump, sit, ask* . . . Rather boring, possibly. In fact, verbs have a great deal of hidden power, because they can change their form in many different ways, and thus express many different meanings. In particular, there are changes in form which help us to talk about the *time* at which an action takes place, and these are called the verb's **tenses**. In English, there are just two tenses where the verb changes form in this way. There's the **present tense**, where the verb hasn't any ending at all:

I hop   I skip   I run

And there's the **past tense**, where we add the ending *-ed* or alter some other part of the word:

I hopped   I skipped   I ran

But that's not the end of the story. Many grammar-book writers use the term **tense** to include various other ways in which verbs are able to refer to time. For instance, when *will* or *shall* is used in front of a verb, to talk about future time, they call this the **future tense**: *I will hop* or *I shall hop*. And when *have* is used in front of the verb, to talk about time in the recent past, they call this the **perfect tense**: *I have hopped*. There are other possibilities, too.

GOVERNMENT WORD WARNING! Just because a verb is in the present tense doesn't mean to say that it always refers to present time. Take *Tracy's going to China next year*. Here, the travelling definitely hasn't happened yet, but the verb is in the present tense. Nor does the past tense always refer to past time: in *I was going to London tomorrow – but I'm not now*, the travelling is in the future, but the verb is in the past tense. Tenses turn out to be cunning things, when you start studying them, and aren't boring at all.

 verb   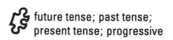 future tense; past tense; present tense; progressive   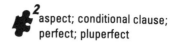 aspect; conditional clause; perfect; pluperfect

thesaurus (thuh-**saw**-ruhs)

You are coming to the end of the best homework essay you've ever written – *you* think! It's about Julius Caesar. You're about to write: 'His main fault was that he was a very proud man', when you stop. You've just used the word 'proud' in the previous sentence. In fact,

I'm a **thesaurus**......
uneatable, unappetising,
inedible, unpalatable,
distasteful, disagreeable...

you've used it twice in the same paragraph already! You don't want to use it again. What's another word for *proud*? Your mind goes blank. You've only got five minutes before *Neighbours*, and then you're going out. You've got to finish the essay. What's another word for *proud*? Help!

Don't panic. All you have to do is look *proud* up in a **thesaurus**. (What's that? You haven't got one? Check that out. The best-known one is called *Roget's Thesaurus*, named after the nineteenth-century writer, Peter Mark Roget – pronounced **ro**-zhay. There may well be one in the house and you don't know it's there. If there isn't, put one on the next shopping list, use *proud* a third time, and be satisfied with a mark of 9½ out of 10.) A thesaurus isn't a dictionary. In a dictionary, you have a particular word in mind, and you want to find out its meaning, or spelling, or whatever. In a thesaurus, you have a particular meaning in your mind, and you want to find out what words there are in the language which have that kind of meaning.

What you do is this. Look up the meaning in the index at the back of the thesaurus – let's take *proud*. The index sends you to a particular page, and there you'll find many of the words which express the meaning of pride – words like *arrogant*, *vain*, *haughty*, *big-headed*, and several more. You can then choose one which you think will do the job. Of course, you may need to look these words up in a dictionary first, to find out what they mean. A thesaurus doesn't give you dictionary information, such as meanings and pronunciations.

Armed with a good dictionary and a good thesaurus, you'll be able to cope with almost anything in the world of words. And watch *Neighbours* as well.

 vocabulary    dictionary; synonyms    concordance

topic sentence

I thought I'd let you know that I'm writing my latest great work of science fiction. I've reached the point where Dr Which (a relative of Dr Who) is being attacked by a gang of Lects from the planet Argot. I need to write a short paragraph telling you how bad the attack is. That's my theme, or **topic**, for the paragraph. So I must make sure that one of the sentences makes it clear that this is what the paragraph is about. I think I'll have *Dr Which had never experienced an attack of such ferocity on the small ship*. Then I'll tell you a bit more about what the attack was like. In other words, I've told you my **topic sentence** – the sentence that tells you most about what the paragraph is about.

The only problem is: I can't decide where to put my topic sentence. Should it be at the beginning, like this?

Dr Which had never experienced an attack of such ferocity on the small ship. There was a booming in his ears, and his brain felt as if it would burst. The walls of the cabin were vibrating, and cracks were beginning to appear in the outer protective casing. He could dimly see the precious safety lock fluid seep out of its shell. Only one defence seal left!

Or at the end, like this?

Dr Which heard a booming in his ears, and his brain felt as if it would burst. The walls of the cabin were vibrating, and cracks were beginning to appear in the outer protective casing. He could dimly see the precious safety lock fluid seep out of its shell. Only one defence seal left! He had never experienced an attack of such ferocity on the small ship.

Or in the middle, like this?

Dr Which heard a booming in his ears, and his brain felt as if it would burst. The walls of the cabin were vibrating, and cracks were beginning to appear in the outer protective casing. He had never experienced an attack of such ferocity on the small ship. He could dimly see the precious safety lock fluid seep out of its shell. Only one defence seal left!

I can put my topic sentence anywhere I like. Most writers put it at or near the beginning of the paragraph, but sometimes it's more effective later on. What do *you* think?

 paragraph    discourse; text

transitive verb (**tran**-zi-tiv verb) and
intransitive verb (in-**tran**-zi-tiv verb)

DAVE: Hey, Phil.
PHIL: What?
DAVE: I've just heard a fascinating fact from Number 1.
PHIL: What is it?
DAVE: Some verbs take objects, and some verbs don't.
PHIL: Cor. I'll pass it on.

Not a very likely conversation, I admit – but then Dave and Phil *are* in a Home For Grammarians Who Have Lost Their Marbles, so it's not too surprising. (They found it difficult to get in, actually, as there's a long waiting list.) However, they are quite correct. Some verbs do take objects: they're called **transitive verbs**. Some verbs don't: they're called **intransitive verbs**. Here are some transitive verbs (I've put a typical object in brackets):

find (my diary)   like (my book)   want (an egg)

And here are some intransitive verbs:

come   wait   happen   fall   rise

We say things like *They're coming*, *The car's waiting*, and *I'm falling*. Now, notice what happens if you try to use the transitive verbs without their object:

*I like.   *I found.   *You want.

You get sentences that aren't acceptable in English (as shown by the asterisk). You have to want *something* or like *something*. And notice what happens if you try to use the second set with an object:

*happen an accident   *fall a book   *wait the train

Again, you get some unacceptable sentences. So, as at least one verb turns up in almost every English sentence, you'll gather that it's pretty important to know about the difference between transitive and intransitive. Maybe Dave and Phil were right to be excited, after all.

 object; verb

underextension (uhn-duhr-eks-**ten**-shuhn)

'What have you got on your feet?', I asked Simon, aged two. 'Shoes,' he said. 'That's right,' I said. 'And I've got shoes on my feet, too. Look!' Simon looked, but seemed puzzled. 'Where are my shoes, Simon?', I asked. No reply. 'Where are *your* shoes, then?' He pointed towards his feet. I pointed at my feet. 'Have I got shoes on?' 'No,' he said.

What's going on here? Does Simon understand the word *shoes* or doesn't he? The answer is: something in between. He seems to think that *shoes* is the name of just *his* shoes. He hasn't yet learned that the word *shoes* applies to all kinds of shoes on all kinds of feet. Putting this another way, Simon hasn't 'extended' the meaning of the word sufficiently. And when a child's word doesn't have as wide a range of meaning as the adult's word, it's called **underextension**.

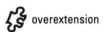 overextension

ungrammatical see **grammar**

upper case and lower case

For many years, when books were printed, the printers used to form the lines of print one letter at a time. A piece of metal with a letter on it would be taken from a box and put in position on the line. In fact, there were two boxes, or **cases** – one above the other. The case higher up held all the capital letters, so these came to be called **upper-case letters**. The case lower down held all the small letters, so these came to be called **lower-case letters**. These days, it's all done by computers, of course, but the two terms have stuck, and we still talk about upper-case and lower-case letters. There's an everyday name for upper-case letters. I've already used it in this entry: they're the **capital letters**. But there isn't an everyday name for the lower-case letters. People sometimes call them 'small' letters or 'ordinary' letters, but such names are very misleading. After all, if you think about it, you can have small capital letters (such as in a newspaper column) and large ones (such as in a newspaper headline). So you'll find the terms upper case and lower case to be quite useful, when you're describing the written language.

 alphabet

usage (**yoo**-sij)

JILL: I spell *encyclopedia* with an *e* in the middle.
PHIL: I spell *encyclopaedia* with an *ae* in the middle.
WILL: I don't know how to spell *encylocpeedia*.

I'm afraid Will's got some homework to do, but Jill and Phil are *both* correct. Phil has learned to spell the word using the spelling which has been used in Britain for a long time. Jill has learned the spelling which has been used in America for a long time, and which is now increasingly used in Britain. Both ways of spelling these words are acceptable. Some educated people use the first spelling; others use the second. Some publishing houses advise their authors to use the first spelling; others advise the second. What we have here, in short, is a difference in **usage** – two different ways of using the language, both of which are widespread.

All areas of language show usage variations. People vary in the way they pronounce certain words: for instance, some pronounce *ate* to rhyme with *late*, and some pronounce it to rhyme with *let*. They vary in their grammar: some prefer to say *I shall run*, whereas others prefer *I will run*. And they vary in their choice of vocabulary, too: some people go to the *toilet*, some go to the *lavatory*, and some go to the *loo*. There are thousands of usage variations in English. I doubt whether any two people speak or write the language in exactly the same way.

 appropriate; correctness; grammar; variety

variety (vuh-**rie**-uh-tee)

MRS P: I don't go to our local greengrocer's very much. There's not much variety.

MRS Q: What a pity. *Our* local shop's got a splendid variety of fruit in this week.

You can see what *variety* means in everyday speech: it means 'a range of different kinds of something'. Fruit and veg, in the case of the greengrocer. In language, a **variety** is a particular kind of speech or writing that you find in a particular situation – a style which belongs to that situation. It's also sometimes called a **register**. For instance, lawyers in court speak in a special way to the judge: they're using the variety (or register) of legal English. Cricket and football reporters on the radio speak in a special way when they're describing a match: they're using the variety of sports commentary. Newspaper reporters write in a variety called journalese. People on posh occasions use the variety of formal speech. Friends talking on everyday occasions use the variety of informal speech. There are hundreds of varieties in English – American and British, north and south, male and female, upper-class and lower-class, specialised and everyday . . . Some are highly distinctive; others are less so. But one thing's clear. The language shop's got a splendid variety, too.

appropriate; dialect; formal; style

verb

There are all kinds of bits and pieces in a sentence, but I doubt if there's anything more important than the verb. The verb is the element which makes everything hold together. If I write down a list of nouns, they won't make much sense by themselves:

Hella Brendan measles

But if I add the verb, suddenly everything's clear.

Hella gave Brendan measles.

There are thousands of verbs in English, and you can divide them into two kinds. Most of them are verbs with a clear meaning, such as *run*, *give*, and *argue*. Then there are a few verbs which work along with these to slant the meaning in various ways, such as *might*, *can*, and *is*. Here are two sentences where both kinds of verb are present:

Hella has given Brendan measles.   Hella might give Brendan measles.

In such sentences, *give* is called the **main verb** and *has* and *might* are called the **auxiliary verbs**. (There's a separate entry on auxiliary verbs, which you should look up as soon as you can.) The main verbs convey two chief kinds of meaning. Most of them express an action or an event: *run*, *jump*, *give*, and *argue* are like this, and so are *write*, *sneeze*, *kick*, *stop*, *snow*, *drink*, and *die*. The others express no actions at all, but rather states or qualities of being: these include *live*, *stand*, *sit*, *have*, *be*, *seem*, *think*, *feel*, and *own*. Can you feel the difference? If someone says *I'm jumping*, you can see the action taking place. But if someone says *I own a Porsche*, you can't see any action in the speaker. So, people who tell you that 'a verb is an action word' aren't telling you the whole story.

parts of speech   auxiliary verb; tense

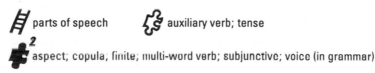

aspect; copula; finite; multi-word verb; subjunctive; voice (in grammar)

verb phrase

Edward cheats.
Edward doesn't cheat.
Edward doesn't have to cheat.
Edward doesn't have to try to cheat.
Edward doesn't have to keep on trying to cheat.

I think that's enough – though I could go on, increasing the length of the phrase following *Edward*. It's a phrase based on the word *cheat*. *Cheat* is a verb. So we call the construction a **verb phrase**. Here are some other verb phrases which I'm using in this entry:

could go on   'm using   can see   can be   want to see

Most verb phrases, as you can see, are much shorter than the ones at the top of the entry. Usually, verb phrases consist of only two or three words. (That makes them very different from noun phrases, which can be extremely lengthy. Look at the entry on **noun phrase** if you want to see how it's done.)

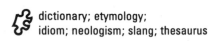 phrase; verb   noun phrase

vocabulary (voh-**kab**-yoo-luh-ree)

Here are two questions that no one knows the answer to. How many words are there in English? And how many English words do you know? These are both questions about the **vocabulary** of English. (The vocabulary is also sometimes called the **lexicon** – from the Greek word for 'word'.) I suppose the simplest answer is to say 'a lot' to both. There must be well over a million words in English as a whole, when you think of all the dialects all round the world and all the scientific words that exist. That total will be far greater, of course, if you include proper nouns (there's a separate entry on **proper noun**, if you don't know what these are). As for the number of words educated people know, I should be surprised if it were less than 50,000. They might only actively use a few thousand of these in everyday speech, but they'd know many more. It doesn't take long, in fact, to get a good score, when you start counting vocabulary. Take the present entry, for instance. How many *different* words are there in it? 30? 50? 75? Actually, there are 106.

dictionary; etymology;
idiom; neologism; slang; thesaurus

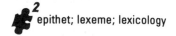² epithet; lexeme; lexicology

wh-question see **question**

word

Here's a question you'll never get on *Mastermind*. What's a **word?** Sounds too easy, I expect you're thinking. In fact, it's quite a difficult question to answer. You'll see why, if you read on. (If you don't feel like a difficult answer, I suggest you read the entry on **word games** instead!)

The *easy* answer is this: a word is the smallest piece of language you can have which has a space on either side. So, there are 12 words in the sentence you are reading now. Some of them are small (such as *in*), and don't have any parts except for the letters which make them up. Others are a bit bigger, and break down easily into parts – such as *words* (*word* + *s*) and *reading* (*read* + *ing*). (There's an entry which tells you about this kind of thing: look up **affix**.) So what's the difficult answer, then? Well, let me put the question this way? How can you tell what a word is in speech? There aren't any neat printed spaces there. In speech, sentences sound something like this:

Ihaveputallthedirtywashinginthewashingmachine.

What are the words here? Here's the way to find out. Read the sentence very slowly, pausing whenever you think it's right to do so. Go on: do it, before you read on. You probably started off like this:

I — have — put — all — the — dirty — washing —

I don't think you will have stopped in the middle of *dirty*, for instance, and said *dir—ty*, or in the middle of *washing*, to say *wash — ing*. Because your brain already knows what the words are, it tells you where to pause – between each one.

So where's the difficulty? The problem comes at the end of the sentence. What did you do after *in the*? Did you say *washing machine*, as if it were one word, or *washing — machine*, as if it were two? In writing it, would you write it as two separate words (*washing machine*) or as one (*washing-machine*)? Whatever you decide, if you try this exercise out in class, you'll find that not everyone agrees with you. The question 'What is a word?' turns out to be tricky after all.

 parts of speech; vocabulary; word games; word order   morphology

word class see **parts of speech**

word games

Here's a piece of research to do next time you've a holiday. Find out all the game shows there are on TV. Every one. When you've done that, work out how many of them are games involving language – **word games**. When I did this, a little while ago, I found that over half the games were to do with words. I don't know whether it's still the same. *Blankety Blank* is one of the most famous, where people are told a phrase, and they have to fill the —. *Call my Bluff* is another one, where people are given an obscure word, and they have to work out which of three possible meanings is the correct one. Then, when people aren't watching television, what do they do? Two of the most popular

136

pastimes are completing crosswords and playing Scrabble. On train journeys you'll see people working their way through fat books of word puzzles. At parties, you can play an enormous number of word games – such as working out how many words you can find in the word *December*. Word games are everywhere. Word games are fun. Words are fun. Language is fun. And, after you finish going through this book, I hope you'll agree with me that studying language is fun.

acrostic; anagram; limerick; palindrome; pangram; rebus; riddle

lipogram; univocalic

word order

You know what they say! *Dog bites postman*. Not news. *Postman bites dog*. Now *that's* news! What you see here is the importance of **word order**. The English language relies on the order of words to get meaning across. Turn a statement into a question? *Jonah is a twit. Is Jonah a twit?* That's word order. Say who did what to whom – as in the *postman* case? That's word order. Most of the rules of English grammar have to do with the order of words, and you can't break those rules – or even bend them, much. Take this sentence:

The red bus arrived at the stop.

Now try putting these words in any other order, to see if you get a possible sentence.

*Bus arrived at the stop the red? No.
*Arrived the red bus at the stop? No.
*Stop at the red bus the arrived? No.
At the stop the red bus arrived? Possibly (in a poem, for instance).

You can see that there's not much room for change. So, word order forget don't the importance of.

 word    grammar; syntax   inversion

yes-no question see **question**

Entries which appear in the Key Stage 4 book

If you have been looking for a language term in this book, and you haven't found it, it will probably be in the Key Stage 4 book. Here is a list of the terms in that book, to help you check. If the term isn't in either book, sorry! Write and tell me what it is, so that I know. There may be a chance to do something about it, one day.

abstract noun *and* concrete noun
active voice *see* voice (in grammar)
affricate
agent
alliteration
allophone
alveolar
anacoluthon / anacolutha
analogy
anapaest *see* foot
animate *and* inanimate
antecedent
aphorism
apposition
approximant
argot
articulation / articulator
aspect
aspiration / aspirated
assimilation / assimilate
assonance
back *see* front
bilabial
cant *see* argot
cardinal numeral *and* ordinal numeral
cleft sentence
click
close vowel *and* open vowel
cluster
coherence / coherent
cohesion
collective noun
collocation
comment clause
complex sentence
compound sentence

concordance
concrete noun *see* abstract noun
conditional clause
connotation *see* denotation
consonant *and* vowel
context
contour
copula
corpus / corpora
count noun *and* non-count noun
creole
dactyl *see* foot
declarative
demonstrative
denotation *and* connotation
dental
determiner
deviance / deviant
diacritic
digraph
diphthong
discourse
echo utterance
-ed form *see* participle
elision / elide
ellipsis / ellipses / elliptical
emotive meaning
epigram *or* epigraph
epithet
euphony / euphonious
existential sentence
expansion
expletive
eye rhyme
finite *and* nonfinite
focus

foot
foregrounded / foregrounding
free direct speech *and* free indirect speech
fricative
front *and* back
generic reference
given *and* new
glottis / glottal
grapheme
graphology
group genetive
haiku
head
high vowel *see* close vowel
historic present
holophrase
homographs *see* homonyms
homonyms
homophones *see* homonyms
hyperbole
hypernyms *see* hyponyms
hyponyms / hyponymy
iambic foot *see* foot
ideogram
idiolect
imperative
impersonal style
inanimate *see* animate
incoherence *see* coherence
indefinite pronoun
indicative
inference / infer
informant
ing-form *see* participle
intensifier
International Phonetic Alphabet
interrogative
intonation
intrusive r *see* linking sound
inversion / invert
IPA *see* International Phonetic Alphabet
irony / ironic
irregular
labial
labio-dental
larynx
lateral

lexeme
lexicography *see* lexicology
lexicology
lingua franca
linguistics
linking sound
lipogram
litotes
low vowel *see* close vowel
major sentence *and* minor sentence
malapropism
mass noun *see* count noun
metalanguage / metalinguistic
metonymy / metonym
mid vowel *see* close vowel
minimal pair
minor sentence *see* major sentence
modal verb *see* mood
modify / modification
mood
morpheme *see* morphology
morphology
multi-word verb
nasal
new *see* given
non-count noun *see* count noun
nondefining clause *see* restrictive clause
nonfinite *see* finite
nonrestrictive clause *see* restrictive clause
onomatopoeia *see* sound symbolism
open vowel *see* close vowel
oracy
ordinal numeral *see* cardinal numeral
orthography
oxymoron / plural oxymora
palate / palatal
paradox / paradoxical
parallelism
parenthesis / parentheses / parenthetic
parody / parodist
parsing
participle
particle
partitive *see* quantifier
passive voice *see* voice (in grammar)
perfect
personal style *see* impersonal style

pharynx / pharyngeal
phoneme
phonetics / phonetician
phonology / phonologist
phrasal verb *see* multi-word verb
pidgin
plosive
pluperfect
polysemic / polysemy
possessive
postmodify / premodify *see* modify
prosody / prosodic
quantifier
Received Pronunciation
reflexive pronoun
regular *see* irregular
relative
restrictive *see* nonrestrictive
rhetorical question
roll *see* trill
rounding / rounded
RP *see* Received Pronunciation
sarcasm *see* irony
semi-vowel *see* approximant
sibilance / sibilant
sound symbolism
spelling reform *see* orthography
spondee *see* foot

spread *see* rounding
stop consonant *see* plosive
stress
subjunctive
suprasegmental feature
syllable
tag question
tautology / tautologous
text
tone of voice
tongue
transcription *see* phonetic alphabet
transformation
trill
triphthong
trochee *see* foot
unaspirated *see* aspiration
uncountable noun *see* count noun
univocalic
uvula *see* palate
velar
velum *see* palate *and* velar
vocal cords
vocal organs
vocative
voice (in grammar)
voice (in phonetics)
vowel *see* consonant and vowel